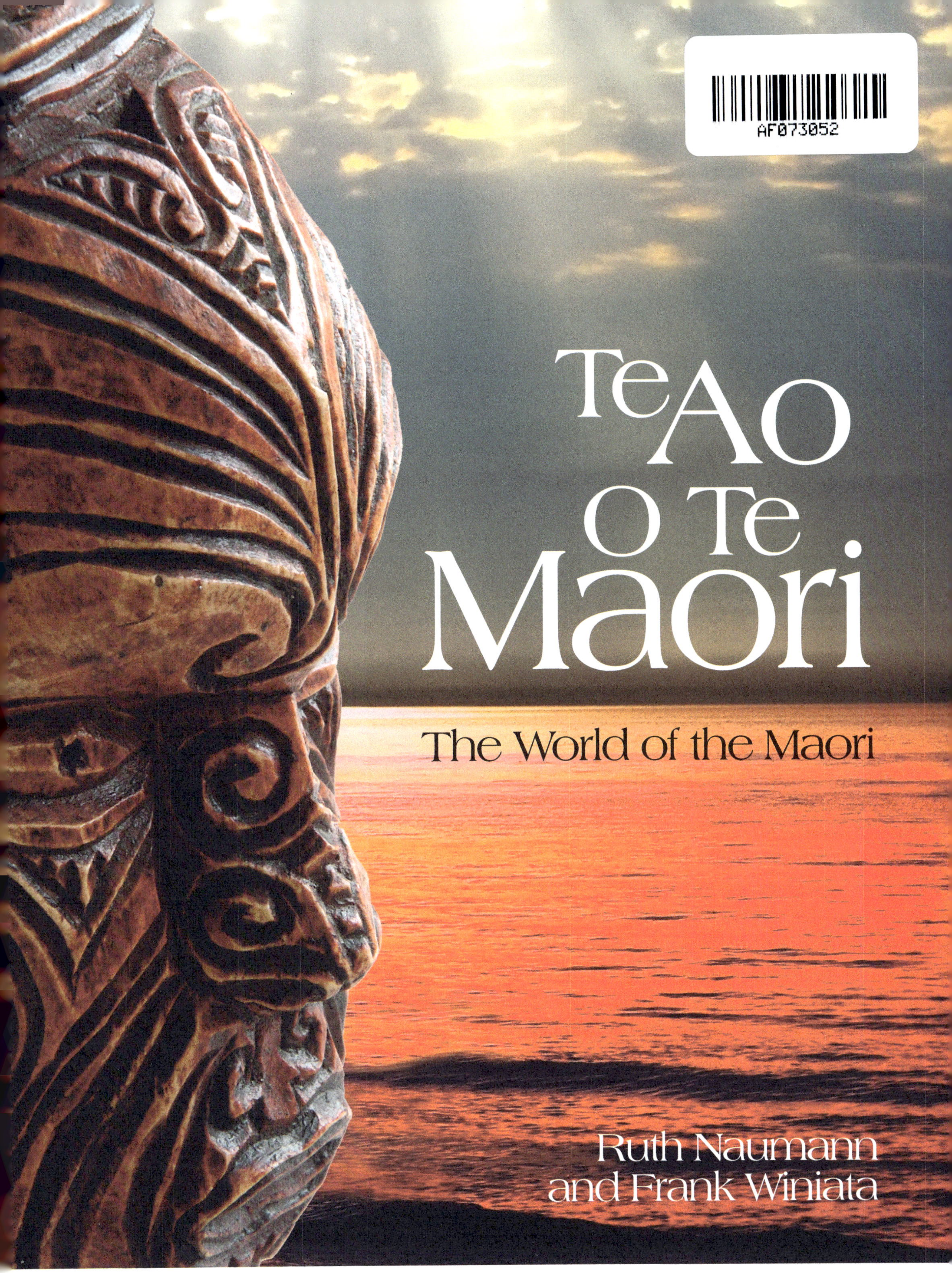

Te Ao O Te Maori

The World of the Maori

Ruth Naumann and Frank Winiata

Australia • Brazil • Japan • Korea • Mexico • Singapore • Spain • United Kingdom • United States

Te Ao O Te Maori
2nd Edition
Ruth Naumann

Cover design: Cheryl Rowe
Text design: Cheryl Rowe
Production controller: Siew Han Ong
Reprint: Jess Lovell

Any URLs contained in this publication were checked for currency during the production process. Note, however, that the publisher cannot vouch for the ongoing currency of URLs.

First published as Te Ao o Te Maori
First published in 1990 by New House Publishers

Acknowledgements
Laurence Clark for illustrations on pages 4, 5, 7, 14, 16, 17, 18, 19, 22, 23, 26, 32, 43, 45. Shutterstock for the cover image, photograph by Jamie Thorpe. NZ Post for the postage stamp images on page 6. Auckland Art Gallery for the painting on page 10: Charles F Goldie, Louis John Steele The Arrival of the Maoris in New Zealand, 1898 oil on canvas, gift of the late George and Helen Boyd.
The Alexander Turnbull Library, National Library of New Zealand, Te Puna Matauranga o Aotearoa for page 13, Dittmer, Wilhelm, 1866-1909 : Hawaiki. [London, Routledge, 1907], Reference No. PUBL-0088-095; page 15, Skull of kuri (native dog) found at Roha-a-te-kawau island pa, Horowhenua district. 2 October 1932
Reference No. PA1-f-009-285; page 21, Backhouse, John Philemon, 1845 -1908 :[Maori village scene. ca 1880] Reference No. E-053-012; page 28/29; [Clark, Russell Stuart] 1905-1966 :Working in the kumara plantation [1955] Reference number: B-023-017; page 28, Heaphy, Charles 1820-1881 :Wata or Provision house, at Otumatua on the North shore of Cook's Strait. Drawn by Chas Heaphy Esq.r [1841]. Day & Haghe. London, Smith, Elder [1845], Reference No. PUBL-0011-11; page 30, [Merrett, Joseph Jenner] 1816 -1854 :A feast at Mata-ta, on the East Coast, Mt Edgecumbe in the distance. II. Throwing the spear, the mode of salutation, a party of visitors arriving / George French Angas [delt]; J. W. Giles [lith]. Plate 36. 1847. Reference No. PUBL-0014-36; page 33, R. Chadwick, wearing a korowai, weaving a small flax basket 1921 Reference No. PA1-q-257-30-3; page 33, [Angas, George French] 1822-1886 :Ngeungeu and her son James Maxwell. Plate 3 / George French Angas. W Hawkins. B. W. lithog. 1846. Reference No. PUBL-0014-03; page 34, Gilfillan, John Alexander 1793-1864 :Interior of a native village or "pa" in New Zealand, situated near the Town of Petre, at Wanganui... J.A. Gilfillan, pinxt., E. Walker, lithr. [London] Day & Son [1850] Reference No. C-029-001; page 36, [Robley, Horatio Gordon] 1840 -1930 :Tapu. [1863 or 1864] Reference No. A-080-003; page 39, [Robley, Horatio Gordon] 1840-1930 :Moko and Whakairo. [1864 or later]. Reference number: A-080-012; page 40, [Sainson, Louis Auguste de], b. 1800 :Defrichement d'un champ de patates. Boilly sc. Paris, 1839. Reference No. PUBL-0034-2-387; page 42, McDonald, James Ingram, 1865 -1935 :[Alarm in a Maori pa] 1906. Reference No. NON-ATL-0007; page 44, Maori women, in semi traditional costume, playing a stick game alongside a meeting house. Reference No. 1/2-117036-F; page 46, Angas, George French 1822-1886 :Maketu house at Otawhao Pah, built by Puatia, to commemorate the taking of Maketu. [1844]. George French Angas [delt]; J. W. Giles [lith]. Plate 25. 1847. Reference No. PUBL-0014-25; page 46, Cousins, Thomas Selby 1840-1897 :Maori rock drawings in Weka Pass, North Canterbury 1876 Reference No. G-391; page 47, Robley, Horatio Gordon 1840-1930 :Erena. [1864?]. Reference number: A-080-009; Tohunga tattooing a Maori woman [ca 1910]
Reference No. 1/4-021668-F; Maori woman weaving taniko [ca 1910] Reference No. PAColl-6075-13; page 48, [Angas, George French] 1822 -1886 :Taranaki or Mount Egmont. War canoe (early morning). Plate 2 / George French Angas. J W Giles lithog. 1846. Reference No. PUBL-0014 -02.
Pages 8 & 9, material about Te Whare Aronui courtesy of Aramahou Ririnui of Tauranga Boys' College.

© 2009 Cengage Learning Australia Pty Limited

Copyright Notice
Copyright: Apart from fair dealing for the purposes of study, research, criticism or review, or as permitted under Part III of the *Copyright Act 1994*, no part of this Work may be reproduced, copied, stored in a retrieval system, or transmitted in any form or by any means without prior written permission of the Publisher. **Copyright Licences:** Should you wish to make multiple copies of parts of this Work, you may apply for a licence through the Copyright Licensing Limited (CLL). You will need to supply a remuneration notice to CLL and pay any fees. These licences are granted subject to strict conditions. For details of CLL licences and remuneration notices please contact CLL at PO Box 331488, Takapuna, North Shore City 0740. Phone 64 9 486 6250, Fax: 64 9 486 6260. Email: cll@copyright.co.nz

For product information and technology assistance,
in Australia call **1300 790 853**;
in New Zealand call **0800 449 725**

For permission to use material from this text or product, please email
aust.permissions@cengage.com

National Library of New Zealand Cataloguing-in-Publication Data
National Library of New Zealand Cataloguing-in-Publication Data

Naumann, Ruth.
Te ao o te Māori = The world of the Māori / Ruth Naumann. 2nd ed.

ISBN 978-017018-224-9
Previously ed: New House Publishers, 1989.
1. Maori (New Zealand people)—History—Juvenile literature.
2. Maori (New Zealand people)—Social life and customs—Juvenile literature. 3. New Zealand—History—To 1840—Juvenile literature.
[1. Maori (New Zealand people)—History. 2. Maori (New Zealand people) —Social life and customs. 3. Maori (New Zealand people) 4. New Zealand—History.] [1. Tikanga. reo. 2. Kōrero nehe. reo.] I. Title.
II. Series: Naumann, Ruth.
993.01—dc 22

Cengage Learning Australia
Level 7, 80 Dorcas Street
South Melbourne, Victoria Australia 3205

Cengage Learning New Zealand
Unit 4B Rosedale Office Park
331 Rosedale Road, Albany, North Shore 0632, NZ

For learning solutions, visit **cengage.com.au**

Printed in Australia by Ligare Pty Limited.
4 5 6 7 8 9 10 19 18 17 16 15

Contents

1	Ancestral Homelands	4
2	The Moriori Story	6
3	Back to the Beginning	7
4	How a House Can Tell a Story	8
5	Searching for Clues	10
6	Polynesian Puzzler	12
7	Arrival by Sea	14
8	The Sea Voyage	16
9	The Earth Mother	18
10	Changes in a New Environment	20
11	Economic Organisation	21
12	Gathering Kai	22
13	Fishing	24
14	Nuku – The Bird Hunter	26
15	Working to Get Food	28
16	Sharing Resources	30
17	Naming the Environment	31
18	Clothes From the Land	32
19	Blood and Bone Groups	34
20	Tapu	36
21	Taonga	37
22	Problem Solving 1	38
23	Problem Solving 2	40
24	Health	41
25	Pa, War, Weapons	42
26	Games and Sports	44
27	Art	46
28	Your Own Enquiry	48

Ancestral Homelands

Focus
- The migration of tangata whenua is important.
- Exploration creates chances and challenges for people, places, and environments.
- Events have causes and effects.
- People move between places, which has results for the people and the places.
- Ideas and actions of people in the past have helped shape people's lives in New Zealand's developing society.

A long time ago and for a long time, Aotearoa/New Zealand was a land with no people. At some time your ancestors, or you, left an ancestral homeland to come and live in New Zealand. People who do this are called immigrants. Immigrants migrate (move) to another place to make a better life for themselves. Maybe they want to escape violence or war. Maybe they want to own a piece of land. Maybe their homeland is too crowded. Maybe they are looking for adventure, or being explorers.

The first immigrants arrived in canoes from a Polynesian ancestral homeland. They settled on the land as tangata whenua – people of the land. They had no written language. Their immigration stories have been passed on orally. These stories show how immigrants survived in Aotearoa. They did so by making changes to their lifestyle and setting up social controls. Social controls are ideas on behaviour covering all things from how weddings were celebrated to how a chief could be fed so that he did not lose his power by touching food. They become the culture – the special ways of acting and thinking – of a place.

Later immigrants arrived in ships and more recently planes. They came from Europe to start with. Later they came from ancestral homelands all round the world.

Immigrants changed their new homeland of New Zealand. Their actions and ideas have survived through the generations to make New Zealand what it is today.

The immigration time line

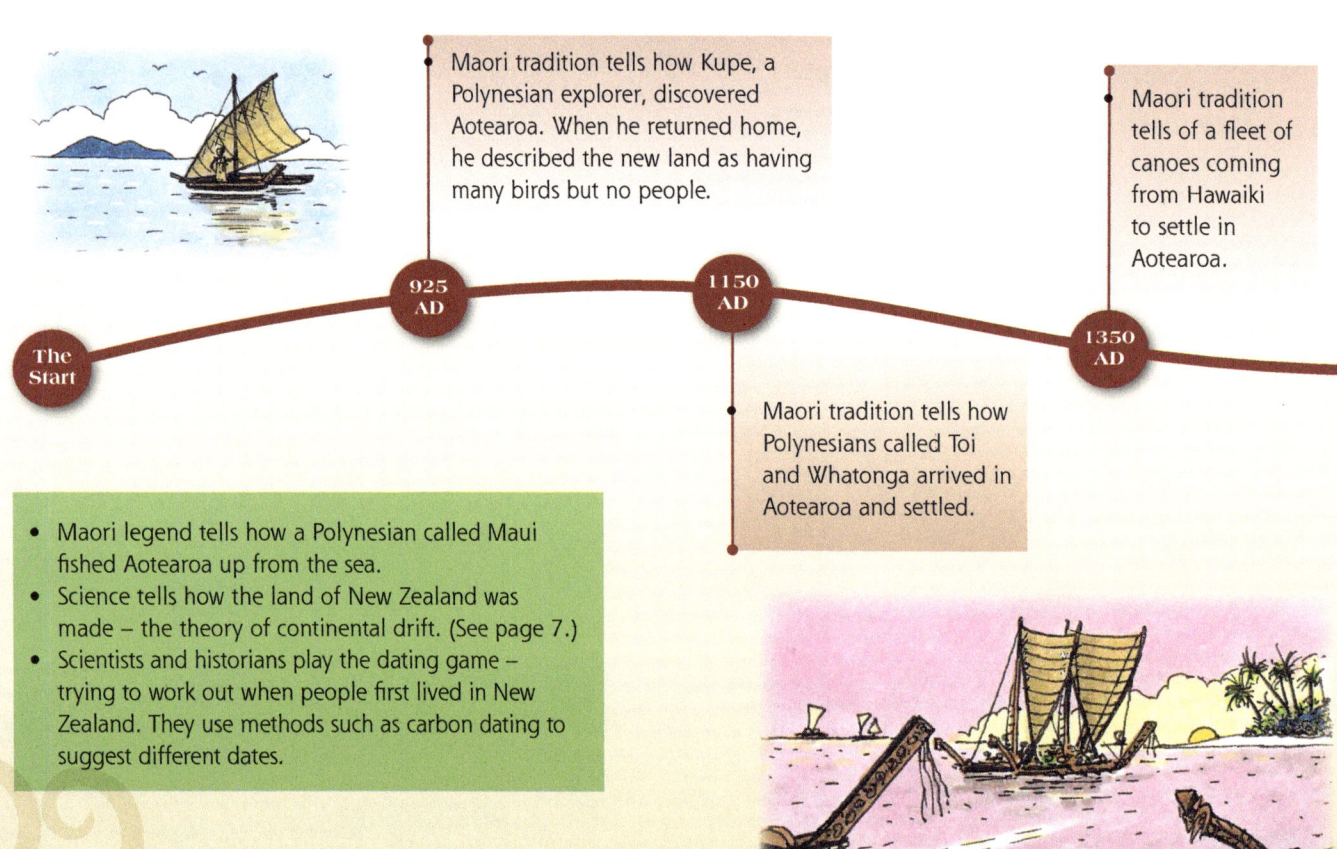

The Start

- Maori legend tells how a Polynesian called Maui fished Aotearoa up from the sea.
- Science tells how the land of New Zealand was made – the theory of continental drift. (See page 7.)
- Scientists and historians play the dating game – trying to work out when people first lived in New Zealand. They use methods such as carbon dating to suggest different dates.

925 AD — Maori tradition tells how Kupe, a Polynesian explorer, discovered Aotearoa. When he returned home, he described the new land as having many birds but no people.

1150 AD — Maori tradition tells how Polynesians called Toi and Whatonga arrived in Aotearoa and settled.

1350 AD — Maori tradition tells of a fleet of canoes coming from Hawaiki to settle in Aotearoa.

Activities

1. Explain what a time line is and why it is a useful method to show information. Describe other methods you could use to show the same information.
2. Make your own copy of The Immigration Time Line (below). Add another two dates for when you were born and for when your ancestors or family came to New Zealand.
3. Find the terms on pages 4 or 5 for the following meanings:
    a) your native land such as country of your birth or country you choose to live in
    b) people of the land, first people in Aotearoa
    c) person from whom you are descended, such as great-grandparent
    d) person from Polynesia, a region of over 1,000 islands in the Pacific Ocean
    e) an agreement between two groups of people
    f) laws passed by Parliament
    g) a country taken over and ruled by another country
    h) by speaking rather than writing
    i) way of finding out the age of things that contain materials that were once alive
    j) ideas and actions of a certain group of people.
4. Research: Find out where the two names of Aotearoa and New Zealand for the same country came from. Also find out different dates suggested for the first people in Aotearoa.

Legend = history story passed down through the generations. Legends can be myths or traditions.

Myth = something that is said to have happened a very long time ago and usually involves the supernatural. Myths, similar to myths in New Zealand, are known in other countries in Polynesia.

Tradition = something that happened closer to the present and involves the natural world. It is a special story just for Aotearoa.

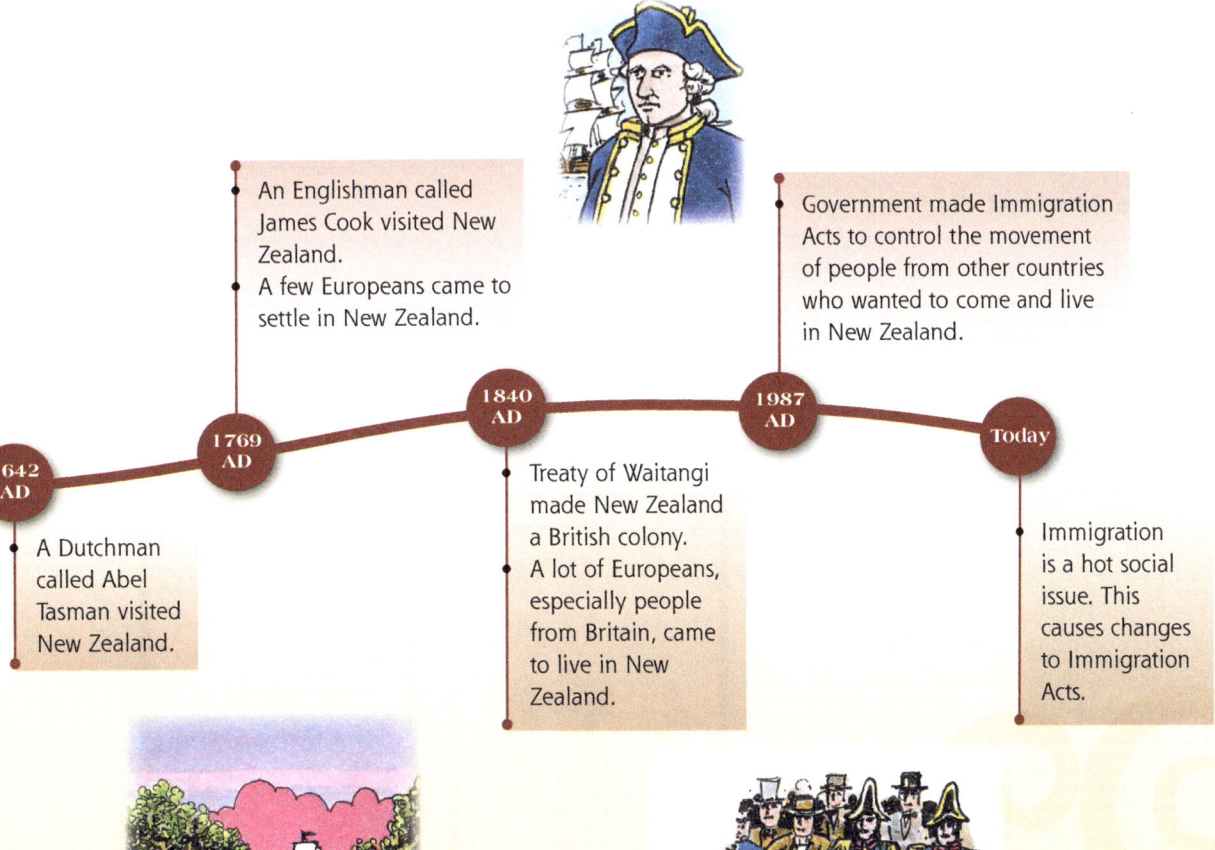

2 The Moriori Story

Focus
- The migration of tangata whenua is important.
- Events have causes and effects.
- Exploration creates chances and challenges for people, places, and environments.
- People move between places, which has results for the people and the places.

VERSION 1 of the story	VERSION 2 of the story
When ancestors of the Maori first came to Aotearoa, a race called Moriori were already living there. Ancestors of the Maori killed and ate the Moriori. The surviving Moriori fled to the Chathams and settled there. There is no evidence to back up this version.	Ancestors of the Moriori are the same people as the ancestors of Maori. At some time between the 9th and 16th centuries, Moriori moved from Aotearoa to live on the Chathams. Current research and archaeological evidence back up this version.

Moriori developed a special culture on the Chatham Islands

Tribes had their own areas.	They lived on fern root, karaka berries, eels, birds, fish, shellfish, seals.	They conserved resources by taking only what they needed.
Seals gave them warm clothes, fat, and meat.	They made tree carvings of human figures or faces.	They practised sustainability (making sure resources did not run out). For example, they killed only old male seals.
Chiefs were chosen for being good at something such as catching birds or fishing.	They made rock carvings of things like seals.	Native trees such as the nikau palm were not suitable for huge ocean-going canoes. Their original canoes rotted away.
They developed the wash-through raft. It had a base of inflated kelp and sides of reeds tied together. As it got partly waterlogged it was more stable in rough seas and high winds. It could go round the islands without capsizing.		
They made trips on rafts to other islands to get albatrosses for food and feathers.	A high-ranking chief ordered that there were to be no more wars between tribes. Any arguments were to stop as soon as blood was drawn. So they became a peaceful people.	

Why Moriori people almost died out
- Europeans arrived in 1791 and whalers and sealers followed. They soon killed all the seals. They killed many birds. They brought diseases for which Moriori had no immunity (protection).
- Maori from two tribes in Aotearoa arrived in 1835. They were tired and sick. Moriori nursed them back to health. The Maori killed many Moriori, claimed a lot of Moriori land, and made other Moriori slaves. The Moriori stayed peaceful and did not fight back. Some died of despair. Tommy Solomon, said to be the last full-blooded Moriori, died in 1933. He is usually shown wearing a hat and carrying a walking stick.

Activities

1. Rule up a page into six boxes of equal size. Head it '40c'. Do the same for a second page and head it '80c'. The six boxes match the six images on each stamp. In each box, explain what the image is about.
2. Make up a chart with the following headings to show actions and results.

Action of non-Moriori in Chathams	Result of action on Moriori

3. Research: Find out another ten important facts about the Moriori.

Back to the Beginning

Focus
- The migration of tangata whenua is important.
- Events have causes and effects.
- Exploration creates chances and challenges for people, places, and environments.
- People move between places, which has results for the people and the places.

Geologists are people who study land. They use theories (ideas) to suggest how New Zealand may have come to be shaped and situated as it is. One theory says that millions of years ago, New Zealand was part of a very large landmass. Geologists call this landmass Gondwana, after a province in India. Very slowly, Gondwana broke up into South America, Africa, India, Antarctica, Australia and New Zealand. These land pieces began to drift away from each other. This is called Continental Drift. New Zealand ended up surrounded by ocean. To the south, there was only Antarctica. This meant:

- people had to get to New Zealand from the north.
- whoever came would have to be very good sailors.
- whoever came would find the forest and forest floor were dense and healthy. This was because New Zealand had drifted away before the time of mammals. Great forests had been able to grow without mammals destroying them.
- whoever came would find a land of birds. Even flightless birds had been able to survive because there were no mammals to eat them.

A more recent idea says it did not happen that way. This idea says New Zealand is the tip of a drowned continent called Zealandia. Zealandia was split off from Gondwana and sank to a depth of one to three km millions of years ago. New Zealand, therefore, has been pushed up from the ocean. All its native plants and animals appeared within the past 23 million years.

The first immigrants were Polynesians – Nga Tamariki A Maui (Children of Maui). They are the ancestors of the Maori. They did not call themselves Maori, which means 'usual' or 'ordinary'. They knew themselves as members of a particular tribe. The next lot of immigrants to arrive were mostly from Europe. They were therefore different to tangata whenua. That was when the term Maori was used.

Maui belongs to many Polynesian cultures including Maori. He had supernatural powers. One day he hauled up a great fish. This is te Ika a Maui or the North Island. The South Island is his canoe. Stewart Island is the anchor.

Activities

1. Explain the difference between a fact and a theory.
2. Describe the difference between the Continental Drift theory and the Zealandia theory.
3. Describe a possible reason for the environment of Aotearoa being different to other places of Gondwana.
4. Research: Find out more about the Zealandia theory of New Zealand rising from the ocean.

How a House Can Tell a Story

Focus
- The migration of tangata whenua is important.
- People remember and record the past in different ways.
- People pass on and look after culture and heritage.
- Exploration creates chances and challenges for people, places, and environments.
- People move between places, which has results for the people and the places.
- Ideas and actions of people in the past have helped shape people's lives in New Zealand's developing society.

Maori have special places in which to store myths and traditions which tell their history. One such place is a whare called the whare wananga, the house of learning. Some schools have whare wananga. An example is Te Whare Aronui at Tauranga Boys' College. Its carvings represent many myths and traditions from three iwi.

The shape of such a whare is also a symbol of an ancestor. When the people are inside, they are sheltered within their ancestor like this:

roof = head   ridgepole = backbone
rafters = ribs   interior = body
barge boards = arms.

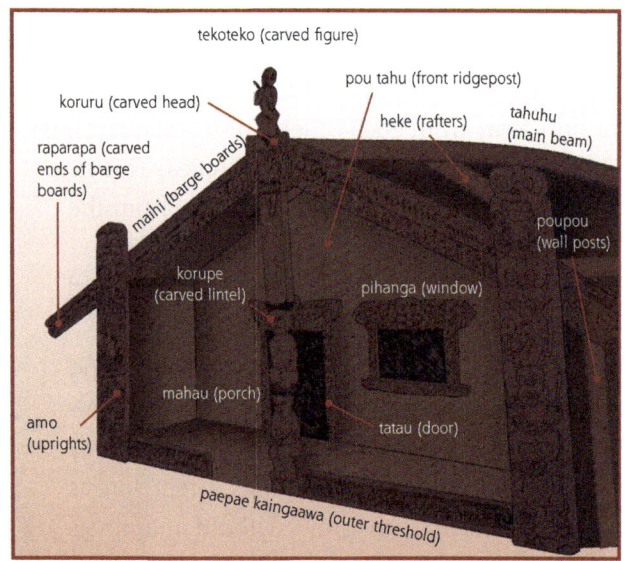

Te Whare Aronui

Aronui's Master Carver and designer was Simon Madgwick. Its carvers were James Tapiata and Tauranga Moana Trustboard Carving Course participants. Like other carved whare standing today, it was built after the arrival of European technology. If it had been built before, it would be much smaller. There would be no glass for the pihanga (window). No nails or iron would have been used. The tatau (door) would be smaller. A fire may have been lit in it to give light and keep people warm. Cooking was not done in the house. But even though materials are modern, the rituals (ways of doings things) and their meanings are unchanged.

What the carvings in Aronui's mahau (porch) say

Amos (two front uprights)
Here are some gods. Rongomatane (god of cultivated foods) has a ko (digging tool) in one hand and a kumara in the other. Haumitiketike (god of uncultivated foods) has a handful of pikopiko (fern shoots). Tangaroa (god of the sea) has a fish in one hand. The art of carving was a gift from Tangaroa and his other hand holds a whao (chisel). Tumatauenga (god of war) holds a toki poutangata (ceremonial adze [an adze is like an axe]).

Tekoteko Aro (middle post)
This is Tane's brother Whiro.

Korupe (carved lintel over the window)
This refers to the settlement of Tauranga Moana by the Nga Marama people.

Poupou (wall posts)
These show the dressing with the stars and soil of Ranginui and Papatuanuku, the first man (Tiki Ahua) and the first woman (Hine Ahuone). They show Maui holding the fish hook, from the jawbone of his ancestor, with which he fished up the land of Aotearoa. Also there is Kupe with Te Wheke-a-Muturangi (octopus) at his feet. One of Kupe's enemies had a pet octopus who got other octopuses to steal bait from Kupe's fishing lines. Kupe chased the octopus all the way to Aotearoa. He finally killed it in Cook Strait. Back in Hawaiki, he told people about the land to the south and gave them sailing directions. The poupou also show first settlement, with an acknowledgement of Maori rock art and the people who were here at this time.

Maihi (barge boards)
These show Tane's quest to get the wananga (knowledge) from Io (supreme being). Io ordered Ranginui and Papatuanuku to choose one of their kind to visit him. Whiro, who was older than Tane, objected to Tane being chosen. Whiro sent a horde of biting and stinging insects to threaten Tane on his journey. Another brother, Tawhirimatea, sent the Aratiatia, his family of whirlwinds, to speed Tane away from the insects. Tane went up through the 12 realms, or heavens. With Io, Tane entered the treasure house Rangiatea. There Tane was given the three baskets of knowledge.

Tekoteko (top figure)
This is Tane. He holds a waka huia (treasure box) representing Te Kete Aronui. This is the basket of war, agriculture, woodwork, stonework and earthwork.

Raparapa (carved ends of barge boards)
These show the other two baskets. Te Kete Tuauri is the basket of peace, goodness and love. Te Kete Tuatea is the basket of prayers, incantations (chants) and rituals.

Paepae (thresholds)
They show Te Kore (the nothingness), Te Po (the dark), Te Ao Marama (the light). Also here is the separation of Ranginui (the sky father) and Papatuanuku (the Earth mother). Papatuanuku is with her unborn child Ruamoko.

Ceiling paintings
These red, black and white patterns are called kowhaiwhai.

Pare (carved lintel over the door)
The central figure is Toi-Kai-Rakau. The other figures are Awanui-a-Rangi and Rauru, important ancestors. The pare represents further settlement, the arrival of Toi and his people, and their settlement of areas in Aotearoa.

Carvings inside Aronui
The ariki (high-ranking) of various waka are represented, along with some of the tohunga (skilled people, priests), hoa wahine (wives), and uri (descendants). They are carved in styles fitting to the waka or geographical area of Taranaki, Te Arawa, Tai Rawhiti, Taitokerau, Poutahu, Tainui, Takitimu, Mataatua. An example of the many other carvings is Mauao, which is the name given to Mount Maunganui. Mauao was once a nameless mountain, one of three mountains together. The others were Otanewainuku and Puwhenua. The nameless one was in love with Puwhenua but she loved Otanewainuku. Broken-hearted, the nameless one decided to drown himself. He was hauled by the patupaiarehe (fairy folk) towards the ocean. However, the sun's first rays fixed him in his present position and gave him his name which means 'caught by the dawn'. He is the symbol of the tribes of Te Moana o Tauranga. Another carving is Manawahine which shows the power and special qualities of females. The figure is Whakahinga.

Activities

1. List all the names mentioned. Include tribes and canoes. Tick the ones you have heard of.
2. Make a sketch of yourself inside a meeting house. Put words around yourself to show how you feel.
3. Draw Maui's fish using these directions: wings = Cape Taranaki and East Cape, tail = Northland, head = Wellington, mouth = Palliser Bay, hook = Hawke's Bay, hole made by hook = Lake Taupo. Describe your drawing.
4. Discuss:
    a. Is it just coincidence that giant octopuses and squids have been found in Cook Strait?
    b. How could Polynesians, who had no geological maps of Aotearoa, have pictured the fish shape of the North Island?
    c. Is it right to say that a person who discovers new islands fishes them out of the blue?
    d. Is it possible people were already in Aotearoa by the time Kupe reported that only birds lived here? How could this be explained?
    e. Do you know any more legends, especially ones from round your area?
5. Research: Find out about local whare and marae.

5 Searching for Clues

Focus
- The migration of tangata whenua is important.
- Exploration creates chances and challenges for people, places, and environments.
- Events have causes and effects.
- People move between places, which has results for the people and the places.
- Ideas and actions of people in the past have helped shape people's lives.

Historians and scientists try to find answers to six questions about events, or happenings, from the past:

What? Example: What happened when the first people came to Aotearoa?
When? Example: When did they come?
Where? Example: Where did they come from?
Who?   Example: Who came?
Why?   Example: Why did they come?
How?   Example: How did they come?

This famous painting of 1898 by Louis Steele and Charles Goldie is called 'The arrival of the Maoris in New Zealand'. Some people say the first arrivals may not have been so under-fed and exhausted. However, everyone agrees that the first people came by canoe. They could not have swum. Planes had not been invented. Polynesians were excellent sailors and builders of travelling canoes. Maori traditions tell of canoes. So it is safe for researchers to say they know how people came.

The first people left no written records. Therefore researchers look for clues about *when* people first arrived.

CLUE 1

Maori call Pacific rats kiore. They were a food source for early Maori. They were not in Aotearoa before people. They are poor swimmers. The only way they could have come is by canoe. Maybe Polynesians brought them on purpose. Or maybe the rats stowed away. Researchers love finding rat bones. These finds are great clues. They can be radiocarbon dated.

Radiocarbon dating helps researchers find out how old things are. Every living thing contains a radioactive form of carbon. When the thing dies, the carbon decays at a known rate. Scientists measure the amount of carbon left. This tells them the age of the thing.

To start with, radiocarbon dating suggested people were in Aotearoa around 1000 – 1100 AD. Then a scientist said radiocarbon dating of rat bones showed people were in Aotearoa around 50 – 150 AD. However, recent radiocarbon dating of rat bones says people first arrived about 1280 – 1300 AD.

CLUE 2 Rats liked to eat land snails. They gnawed and damaged the shells too. Scientists have found that shells before about 1250 show no signs of rats gnawing them.

CLUE 3 Scientists have also examined native seeds that have rat bites on them. The seeds were preserved in peat and swamp. Scientists say the seeds with the bites appeared only after about 1280.

CLUE 4 Mount Tarawera is in the middle the North Island. In 1150 AD it exploded. The explosion was so big it threw volcanic ash over most of the island. Researchers have never found any Maori belongings such as tools under that volcanic ash. They say this suggests Maori were not living in Aotearoa, or the North Island at least, before 1150.

CLUE 5 Pollen is the yellowy powder found in flowers. Some pollen gets preserved in sediment (layers of material like sand and dirt) in places like peat bogs or lake beds. Scientists can see sudden changes in types of pollen in different sediment layers. These changes show forest was cleared by fires. Scientists have found that pollen from some North Island places suggests changes happened around 1280. They know early settlers burned forest. The settlers needed land to make kumara plots and places for houses. Fire also encouraged bracken fern to grow. Early Maori ate the underground stems of the bracken. Researchers can not say for certain that it was people who started the fires. But they wonder if early settlers began lighting fires just after they arrived.

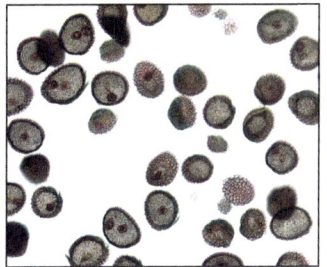

Researchers still can not say exactly *why* the first people came to Aotearoa. Some ideas are:
- They wanted adventure.
- They were looking for places to trade with.
- They wanted to escape overcrowding in their homeland.
- They were visiting another island, got blown off course, drifted, and discovered Aotearoa by accident.
- They wanted to escape arguments over food and land in their homeland. Maybe a toxin was destroying their fish.
- They were banished from their homeland and sent into exile.
- They were looking for new land which would have new resources such as fish and birds.
- They knew the sailing directions to Aotearoa and decided to leave their homeland and settle in Aotearoa.
- They were curious about what lay south of their homeland.
- They wanted to escape war in their homeland.
- They wanted to become heroes who discovered new lands.

Activities

1. Explain the link between the following:
   a) radiocarbon dating and scientists
   b) Pacific rats and land snails
   c) Mount Tarawera and 1150 AD
   d) sediment and pollen
   e) bracken fern and fire.
2. Describe how you might use the clues to decide on a possible date for the first people living in Aotearoa.
3. Discuss possible reasons for why the first people came to Aotearoa.
4. Research: Find out more about radiocarbon dating.

Polynesian Puzzler

Focus
- The migration of tangata whenua is important.
- Exploration creates chances and challenges for people, places, and environments.
- Events have causes and effects.
- People move between places, which has results for the people and the places.

From where did the first people in Aotearoa come? This question continues to puzzle researchers.

Maori myths and traditions speak of Hawaiki as the place from which people are born and the place they go to after they die.

Polynesian jigsaw puzzle

Several thousand years ago people sailed into the Pacific Ocean from Asia. They began to settle the islands there. The last islands settled were the far-off points – Hawaii in the north, Easter Island (Rapa Nui) in the east and Aotearoa/ New Zealand in the south.

For a while canoes returned to East Polynesia. They probably had stopovers at Norfolk Island and Kermadec Islands. Once they stopped returning to Polynesia, settlers in New Zealand cut themselves off from the outside world.

New Zealand, being the most southern islands, would have been reached last.

Scientists have done DNA testing of Maori descendants. DNA stands for deoxyribonucleic acid. It stores genetic information about a person. Genetic means to do with genes. The DNA testing shows that the first people came from somewhere in East Polynesia.

The DNA of Maori descendants, and a very few early items, suggest the area in East Polynesia from which the ancestors of the Maori came was the Society Islands, southern Cook Islands and Australes Islands (Tubuai) in French Polynesia.

Maybe the ancestors of Maori did not come from just one place. DNA testing on the Pacific rat in New Zealand traces it back to Society Islands and Cook Islands. DNA from humans suggests at least 70 to 100 females were founding settlers. That means several canoes. The canoes need not have come from the same place.

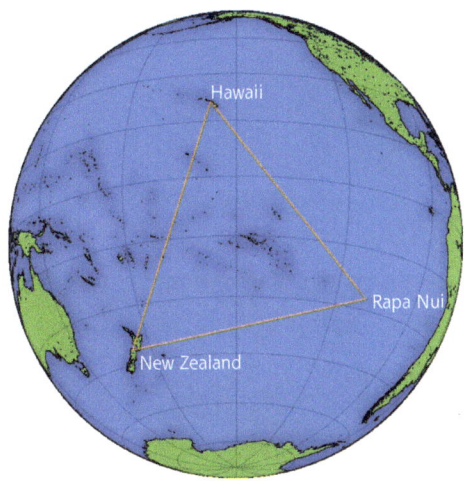

The Polynesian triangle is a region in the Pacific Ocean. Its anchor points are Hawaii, Rapa Nui (Easter Island) and New Zealand.

This drawing from 1907 shows people in Hawaiki waiting to get into canoes and sail away.

Activities

1. Use the clues to work out which island might have been Hawaiki.

A

B

C

D

E

Clues

The word moa is used for the domestic fowl on all islands. Drawings on trees and in caves have been found on all islands except C. People on A, C, and E know the Maui legends. People on those islands and on B are great story-tellers. All islands have remains of double and single-hulled canoes. Native dog skeletons have been found on A and E. The pohutukawa, a name from Hawaiki, grows on all islands. Digging sticks have been found on all islands except B. The Pacific rat is on all islands except E. Colouring and preserving with earth and oil was used on all islands.

2. Discuss whether or not it matters that nobody knows exactly where Hawaiki was.
3. It has been suggested that Hawaiki could be in New Zealand. Explain how that might be possible.
4. Describe what DNA is and how it can help researchers.
5. Research: Find some place-names in New Zealand that are believed to have come from Hawaiki.

Arrival by Sea

Focus
- The migration of tangata whenua is important.
- Exploration creates chances and challenges for people, places, and environments.
- Events have causes and effects.
- People move between places, which has results for the people and the places.
- Ideas and actions of people in the past have helped shape people's lives.

Sailors of the ancient Old Stone Age who sailed among the islands of Asia travelled on rafts. Sailors of the New Stone Age had better technology. They built big canoes. Their canoes could carry plants and animals. It was these voyagers who reached Aotearoa first.

> Old Stone Age and New Stone Age were times in history before people began using metal tools.

Data on Polynesian canoes

- about 20 - 30m long
- built to voyage over deep water
- had crew of about 5 to 15
- could carry women and children
- double-hulled or single-hulled
- sails and paddles
- fibre lashing from plants to hold parts together (there were no nails)
- could sail at speeds of at least 7 knots
- carried food such as kumara, yams, taro, breadfruit, bananas
- carried dogs (kuri) and rats
- carried water in gourds (big fleshy fruit with hard skin, used as containers)
- carried coconuts for food and water
- caught rainwater in canoe sails.

Canoe traditions

- are about the arrival in Aotearoa of Polynesians in canoes
- are also about events that happened before the arrival (such as the voyage)
- are also about events that happened after the arrival (such as exploring the land)
- sometimes have supernatural events such as people arriving on sea monsters
- might have events from more than one voyage
- are important for Maori whakapapa (ancestry) where tribes trace their beginning to an early canoe.

Clever Polynesian navigators

- had no instruments such as compasses so used natural objects like the sun
- set off at dusk
- used landmarks behind them for direction
- followed one star on the horizon until it got too high or disappeared
- then followed another star
- also used the moon and bright planets
- checked the position of the canoe in relation to where the sun rose
- kept the canoe at the same angle to ocean swells
- watched for drifting objects such as seaweed to show current direction
- watched for birds such as gannets that return to nests at sunset
- watched for whales which might lead them to land
- watched the sea for currents, driftwood, whirlpools, fish species, colour change
- watched clouds for signs of land such as high, thick, slow and dark cloud.

Building the canoe

Traditions do not always give a lot of information about the building, and launching, of the canoe. The only tradition that gives much detail is that for the Takitimu. However, even it does not say if the Takitimu was single or double-hulled. These are the steps that made the Takitimu ready.

- The tree trunk was roughly shaped in the forest.
- The trunk was buried to harden the wood and stop it splitting.
- Extra wood was buried for six wash strakes (to form ridge along hull), two masts, sprits (small spars between mast and sail), seats, bow piece, beams for deck, end lengths for hull.
- After several months, the wood was dug up and left in the air and rain.
- All the wood was dragged down to the beach.
- The wood was put in a canoe shed to dry out.
- When the wood was dry, it was trimmed and lashed together.
- The hull was given a coating of tree gum.
- It was painted with red ochre – a mix of shark oil and soil.
- The canoe was floated to test its balance.
- The shelter was put on.
- The men were given their special jobs.
- The provisions were loaded.
- The canoe was launched and men, women and children climbed aboard.
- The navigators set course.

Activities

1. Explain
   a) why sailors of the ancient Old Stone Age did not reach New Zealand.
   b) what information you would use to prove Polynesians were great sailors.
   c) how canoes were made seaworthy.
   d) the link between canoes and Maori whakapapa.
2. Discuss whether the names of canoes, such as Takitimu, should be written in italics or not.
3. Describe why the following were important:
   a) gourds b) ochre c) plant fibre d) gannets e) kuri.
4. Research: Find the names of other ancestral canoes.

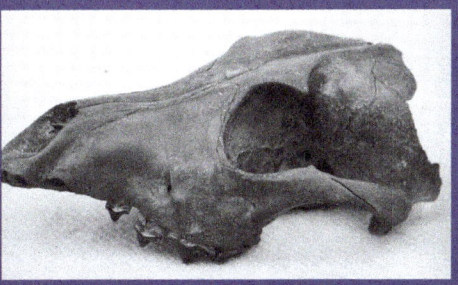

The kuri was the Polynesian dog brought to New Zealand. It was small, long-haired, bushy-tailed, short-legged. It came in various colours such as black, white, yellow. It was used as a food source for early people. It gradually died out.

The Sea Voyage

Focus
- The migration of tangata whenua is important.
- Exploration creates chances and challenges for people, places, and environments.
- Events have causes and effects.
- People move between places, which has results for the people and the places.

Traditions do not say much about the actual voyage. There must have been great dangers. Navigators must have been special people. They would have been trained to study patterns, movements and signs at sea.

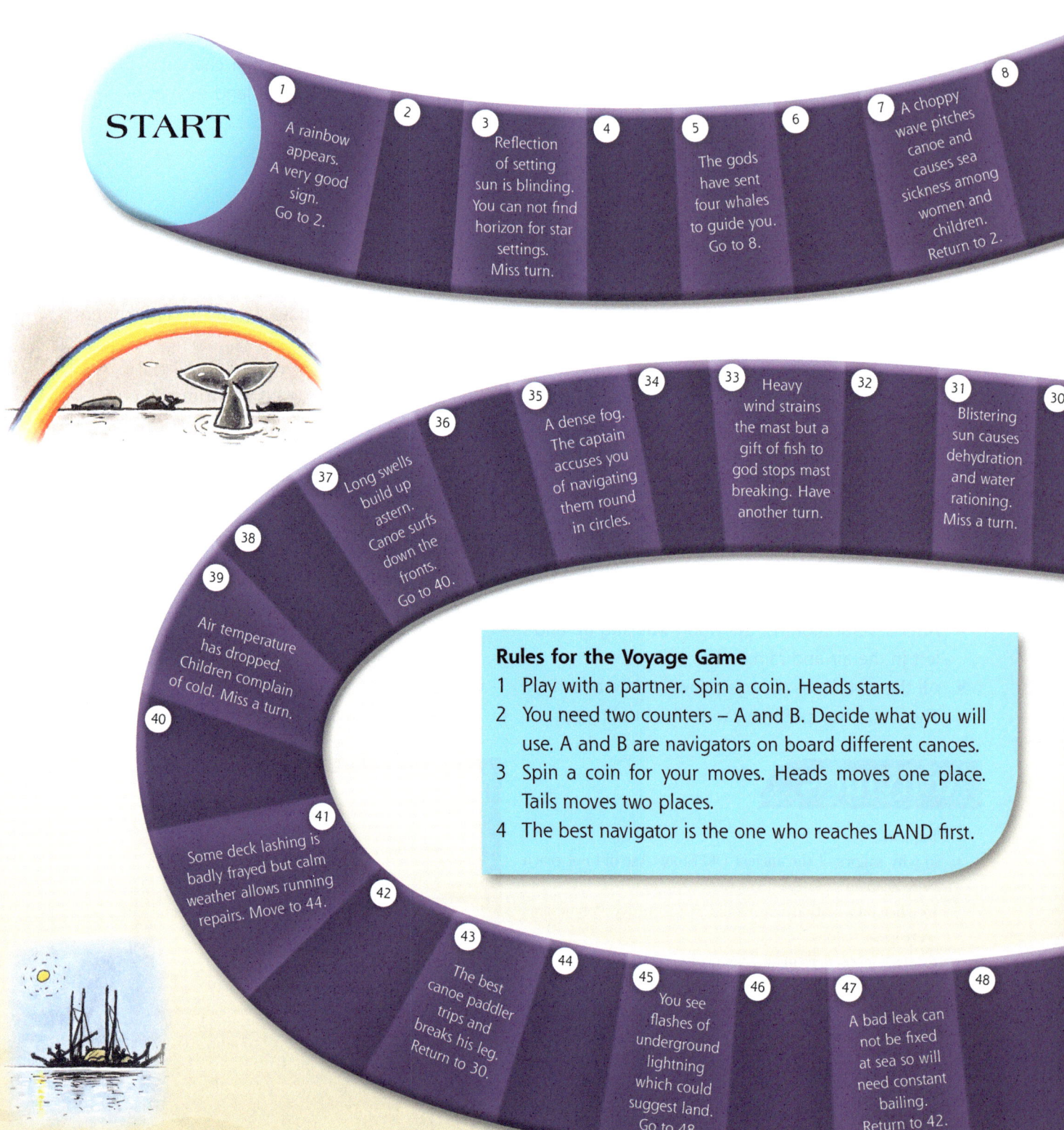

Rules for the Voyage Game
1. Play with a partner. Spin a coin. Heads starts.
2. You need two counters – A and B. Decide what you will use. A and B are navigators on board different canoes.
3. Spin a coin for your moves. Heads moves one place. Tails moves two places.
4. The best navigator is the one who reaches LAND first.

START

1. A rainbow appears. A very good sign. Go to 2.
2.
3. Reflection of setting sun is blinding. You can not find horizon for star settings. Miss turn.
4.
5. The gods have sent four whales to guide you. Go to 8.
6.
7. A choppy wave pitches canoe and causes sea sickness among women and children. Return to 2.
8.

30. Blistering sun causes dehydration and water rationing. Miss a turn.
31.
32.
33. Heavy wind strains the mast but a gift of fish to god stops mast breaking. Have another turn.
34.
35. A dense fog. The captain accuses you of navigating them round in circles.
36.
37. Long swells build up astern. Canoe surfs down the fronts. Go to 40.
38.
39. Air temperature has dropped. Children complain of cold. Miss a turn.
40.
41. Some deck lashing is badly frayed but calm weather allows running repairs. Move to 44.
42.
43. The best canoe paddler trips and breaks his leg. Return to 30.
44.
45. You see flashes of underground lightning which could suggest land. Go to 48.
46.
47. A bad leak can not be fixed at sea so will need constant bailing. Return to 42.
48.

ISBN 978 0170182249

- 10 — Your two sons catch some fish. Go to 14.
- 11
- 12 — A heavy swell forces you to change direction to stop capsizing. Return to 8.
- 13 — You use coconut shells to test drift. Move to 16.
- 14
- 15 — The captain's wife wants to go back home. He threatens to throw her overboard. Return to 12.
- 16
- 17 — A furious storm but your chants calm the waves. Go to 20.
- 18
- 19 — A kuri destroys some of the crops on board. Return to 14.
- 20
- 21 — Two children playing on deck shelter fall overboard but are picked up safely. Move to 22.
- 22
- 23 — Bad gales convince people that voyage is not blessed by gods. Everyone sad. Return to 4.
- 24
- 25 — Your guiding stars are very clear on the horizon. Go to 28.
- 26
- 27 — A shark strike takes the priest's special fishing lure. Return to 16.
- 28
- 29 — A strong current pushes canoe backwards but hard paddling breaks it free. Move to 30.

- 50 — You see ow-moving clouds in he distance. Move to 50.
- 51 — You see a flock of birds fishing. Move to 52.
- 52
- 53 — A string of clear, cloudless days means extra hard paddling. Miss a turn.
- 54
- 55 — Whales come to escort the canoe. Move to Land.

LAND

ISBN 978 0170182249

17

9 The Earth Mother

Focus
- The migration of tangata whenua is important.
- Exploration creates chances and challenges for people, places, and environments.
- Events have causes and effects.
- People move between places, which has results for the people and the places.
- Ideas and actions of people in the past have helped shape people's lives in New Zealand's developing society.

Important facts about the relationship between the first people and their environment

1. The people were tangata whenua – people of the land.
2. In Maori myths, land is an ancestor. It is Papa, the Earth Mother, from whom came Tane and then the Maori people.
3. The people were conservationists. The land gave them everything they needed to survive. In return they made sure the land survived. They killed off some birds such as the moa. However, population was small and the people made no big changes to how the land looked.
4. The lifestyle developed in New Zealand was the most advanced of all the Stone Age cultures within the Polynesian triangle. The environment helped this. Although people had to work for it, there was plenty of food. The people had to invent things. They had to be willing and able to take risks and change their lifestyle.
5. People and environment became tied together. People had love and and respect for their ancestors. They buried ancestors in land, caves or trees. Every feature of the environment in the tribal area became associated with a special memory.
6. If people were captured by another tribe during a battle and made slaves, it was bad enough knowing that if they escaped, they would have lost their mana (standing) with their own tribe. What was worse was that they had been exiled from their land.
7. People did not think of themselves as part of a large Maori society. They thought of themselves as belonging to their family, sub-tribal and tribal groupings. They thought of themselves as belonging to a special area of land.
8. Two important terms that showed this idea are turangawaewae and tangata whenua. The first means a standing place for the feet. It showed that people had rights on some land. This made them tangata whenua on that land. The land gave them identity.
9. It did not matter whether a person was tangata whenua on very fertile, highly cultivated land or on unproductive land.
10. Maori introduce themselves by relating to their land. For example, their marae, tribe, maunga (mountain), awa (river).

FIORDS AND SOUNDS that had steep sides and seemed to cover sunken land.

THERMAL AREAS that were alive with geysers, mudpools, hot springs and steam.

SCRUBLANDS AND FERNLANDS that could survive, along with its birds, because there were no mammals to destroy it.

SWAMPLANDS that had swamp forest along the lower end of rivers where they widened.

SAND DUNES that were huge and ran between beach and forest.

TEMPERATURES that were much colder than what they were used to.

Activities

1. You have been captured by another tribe. The tribe has spared your life. However, you are ill with longing for your own land. Make a sketch of your tribal area. Add the following to it.
   a. The place where an ancestral cheiftaness was killed and eaten by tribal enemies.
   b. The lake where a big taniwha (monster) lives.
   c. The place where the tangata atua (god man), an ancestor of the tribe, changed the path of the river.
   d. The place where the tohunga (priest) sacrificed three slaves to a god.
   e. The place where you saw many stranded whales beached and butchered by the tribe.
   f. The cave that houses the bones of a famous ancestor and is guarded by powerful spirits.

BIRDS that included Haast's eagle, the largest eagle in the world.

MOUNTAIN RANGES that seemed impossible to cross over.

VOLCANOES that had cones or craters and looked as if they might erupt.

SNOW that was something they had never seen before.

ALPINE AREAS that were bare rock and ice.

LAKES that were huge, strange colours and seemed bottomless.

FOREST that was thick and dark, almost all evergreen, with trees like kauri that were giants and very old.

RIVERS that were long, wide and often flooded.

UNDERGROWTH that was thick enough for a kuri to walk on.

SEA MAMMALS such as the seal along the coast.

TUSSOCK GRASSLANDS that housed a flightless bird (moa) that was bigger than them.

ISLANDS that looked like pieces of land a giant had dropped along the coast and then further out to sea.

g   The gorge where there are some healing hot springs.
h   The sacred rock in the middle of the river.
i   The place where your brother got caught up in a hinaki (eel trap).
j   The three big boulders which show where the gods turned people into stones.
k   The place where you think the priest's tuahu shrine (religious place) is hidden.
l   The high mountain peak named after a great warrior chief killed in battle.
m   The forest area you helped clear for the kumara plots.

2   Match the following explanations with the sayings under them.
   a   Aotahi is the wife of Tuterangiwhiu and is the cause of the greatest battle fought in the Waiapu valley.
   b   The people love their land as they love their mother.
   c   Kohere refuses to run away from the approaching war party.
   d   There is twittering of birds but no human voice is heard.
   e   The land gives people their life spirit.

Some Maori sayings which show the importance of land are:
A   Man's blood is food, his substance is land.
B   For land and women, men would die.
C   The land still remains when the people have disappeared.
D   If I must die, le me die on my land.
E   Papatuanuku is man's parent.

3   Research: Find out who Tane was.

Changes in a New Environment

Focus
- The migration of tangata whenua is important.
- Exploration creates chances and challenges for people, places, and environments.
- Events have causes and effects.
- People move between places, which has results for the people and the places.
- Ideas and actions of people in the past have helped shape people's lives in New Zealand's developing society.

The environment of Aotearoa was very different to the tropical island that the Polynesians were used to. The greatest change was the weather. Their new homeland was ruled by seasons and got very cold. This changed their lives.

The environment gave them resources that they could use to survive. However, they had to use all their skills to find solutions to the problems they found.

Some problems and solutions

Problems	Solutions
Used to houses built on raised piles but it is too cold for that here.	LEARN HOW TO STORE CROPS
Used to warm air temperatures all year but here there are long periods of cold and rain.	USE PAUA SHELL
Used to foods like coconut, breadfruit and bananas but it is too cold here for these.	USE SHELLFISH, RIVER FISH, LEARN NEW CATCHING METHODS
Used to paper mulberry tree for making clothes and fabric but it is too cold to grow a big supply here.	USE BONE
Used to making tools from coral but there is no supply here.	USE NIKAU PALM AND RAUPO
Used to coconut leaf walling to let cool winds in but here it is too cold for that.	MAKE RAIN CAPES AND FEATHER CAPES
Used to coral reefs and lagoons for safe fishing but there are none here.	USE INLAND RIVERS AS HIGHWAYS
Used to trade winds for safe sea travel but here winds are seasonal and changeable.	USE TOETOE AND THATCH THICKLY OVER STRONG WALL POSTS
Used to pandanus for roof thatch but it is too cold for it to grow here.	LEARN HOW TO WEAVE FLAX
Used to all-year growing seasons but here it is too cold for more than one crop a year.	FIND OTHERS LIKE FERN ROOT, BERRIES
Used to pearl to decorate tools but there is no supply here.	USE SUNKEN FLOOR LEVELS

Activities

1. Discuss which solution best matches each problem.
2. Tradition says that the Takitimu canoe anchored at what is today called Mauo or Mt Maunganui. The tohunga, captain and crew climbed the hill to thank the gods for their safe arrival. From the hill they would have got a long view of their new homeland. Describe how they might have felt.
3. Research: Find out about raupo and the nikau palm.

Economic Organisation

Focus
- The migration of tangata whenua is important.
- Economic decisions have an impact on people and communities.
- The way people manage resources has an impact on the environment.

Economic = the production, distribution and use of resources such as food.

PROOF A: People settled near food resources. They had no modern technology such as fridges, fishing trawlers, factories producing tinned food. They did not trade with other islands. To start with they settled around harbours or river mouths. Later they shifted inland. There they grew crops and used food from the forests.

PROOF B: Tribes who lived near or in the forest hunted rats and birds from June to September. They caught eels from March to May. Tribes who grew crops in cultivated areas planted in October. In February and March they harvested. At the end of November they began digging fern roots.

PROOF C: Feasts were a fine way to show wealth. The best thing a chief could have was food for guests. This gave the chief, and the tribe, much mana (authority). If a group went past a settlement and did not visit, the people of the settlement felt insulted.

FACTS

1. People had an impact on the environment.
2. Food was what made a tribe wealthy.
3. The environment that a tribe lived in decided when the busy times were.
4. Getting food became the main economic activity.
5. Getting food decided when all other events such as war took place.
6. People admired those who worked hard to produce food.

PROOF D: Raids and battles took place mainly between November and April. A war party would have a better chance of finding food then. However, slaves carried food for warriors even then. At that time food cultivation was easier. Therefore females could cope without warriors to help.

PROOF E: People did not like seeing others being lazy. Many proverbs show this. For example, He kai iana ta te tou e ho ake? (Do you think squatting at home on your backside will bring you food?)

PROOF F: People used the larger animals first. Middens have bones from moa, swans, geese, takahe, penguins, adzebills, seals. Some became extinct. Seals – fur seals and New Zealand sea lions – became extinct in some places. The kiore made some birds extinct. People introduced new plants. They burned forest, perhaps up to 40 percent of it.

Activities

1. Match each fact to a proof.
2. Choose ten inventions that you think would have been most useful to early Maori in their production of food. Explain why you chose each invention.
3. Research: Find the names of some creatures that became extinct in New Zealand before the arrival of Europeans.

Gathering Kai

Focus
- The migration of tangata whenua is important.
- The way people manage resources has an impact on the environment.

OCEAN 5

| START | SHARK AND SHARK OIL | SPOTTY | LING | BLUE COD | RED COD | |

BUSH AND FOREST 6

| MAMAKU (BLACK TREE FERN) Pith and stalks. | HUHU GRUBS | TI (CABBAGE TREE ROOT) Steamed to get sugar crystals. | TI (CABBAGE TREE CENTRE) Cooked as a vegetable. | NIKAU PALM Middle part under leaf is eaten raw. | | GRASSLANDS 20 |

| DUCKS | FRESH WATER CRAYS | | EELS | | MOA |

LAKES 4 — RIVERS 7

| TITIKO (MUD SNAILS) | WATER CRESS | WATER | LAMPREY | | FERN ROOT — This root of bracken fern is a most important food. It grows all year round. Maori dug it up with a pointed stick. They beat it to remove the outer skin. They chewed it or made it into cakes. |
| | | | WHITEBAIT | | PATOTARA PETALS |

FOREST BERRIES 9

Some of these needed careful preparation. The kernel of the karaka berry, for example, is poisonous. It has to be cooked and soaked in water to destroy the poison.

KERERU (WOOD PIGEON)	KARAKA	TAWA	KAREAO SUPPLEJACK	
TUI	HINAU			
KAKA PARROT	RIMU	KAHIKATEA	KAWAKA	COPROSMA
KIWI				POROPORO
KAKARIKI				MAKO
PARAKEET		FOREST BIRDS 15		KOTUKUTUKU
KOPARA (BELL BIRD)	WEKA (WOOD HEN)	GU Resin from kauri tree chewed as gum.	NECTAR from flax, rata, pohutukawa, rewarewa blossoms.	BIRDS' EGGS

		MUSSELS	LIMPETS	PENGUINS	PAUA	CLAMS
	WHALES Did not hunt whales but used stranded whales.		ROCKY COASTS 3			SEALS Maori called them kekeno which means 'look arounds'.
OUTA	SNAPPER					MUTTON BIRDS
						GODWITS
	PARENGO SEAWEED		SEA LETTUCE Eaten fresh or dried, made a good gift.	SEAWEED Bull kelp used as storage bag for food such as mutton birds.	CRAYFISH	ALBATROSS
	KINA SEA EGGS	SHELTERED HARBOURS 1			SANDY BEACHES 2	
	PIPI	COCKLE	PERIWINKLE		TUATUA	TOHEROA
FERN, SCRUB, SWAMPLANDS 8						CRABS
HA	PIKO PIKO SHOOTS Cooked as vegetable.	KIE KIE FRUIT	KIE KIE FLOWERS	RAUPO FLOWER HEADS	RAUPO SHOOTS	
CULTIVATED CROPS 12					MAMMALS 18	
ARA	TARO	YAM	GOURD		KURI DOG	RAT
						BAT Rare and choice food.
						FINISH

Rules for the Gathering Game
1. Play with a partner. Take a turn about. Toss a coin to start. Heads starts.
2. Heads moves two places, tails one place.
3. If you land on a black place you have to give two foods of highest value to your partner. The number in the circle beside the gathering area gives the value of each food from that area.
4. As you play, note down all your landing places.
5. When you have finished, total your score.
6. The winner is the one with the highest score.

Activities

1. Play the Gathering Game.
2. Use the information from the game to draw a full page cross section showing each of the gathering areas and the foods within them.
3. Add these to your cross section: Midden (rubbish pile such as shells), Moa butchery, Tool making site and quarry.
4. Discuss the possible impact on the environment of kai gathering.
5. Research: Find some information on the average life span of early Maori and the state of their teeth.

ISBN 978 0170182249

13 Fishing

Focus
- The migration of tangata whenua is important.
- The way people manage resources has an impact on the environment.
- The ideas and actions of people in the past have had an impact on shaping people's lives.

Modern research shows Maori took over 120 types of fish from the sea. Fresh water fish came from lakes and rivers. Confusion over fish names happens because some fish had more than one name. Also there were different names for different sizes of fish.

Fish such as tamure (snapper), kahawai and parore was eaten fresh or preserved by smoking or drying on rails.

Fishing lines (aho) were made from flax fibre rolled into twisted cord.

Seals were hunted for their meat and skins.

Tribes had their own fishing grounds (tauranga ika). Tribal boundaries were marked out by stakes and landmarks such as headlands.

Tribes guarded knowledge of their tauranga ika. They passed the knowledge down the generations.

Fishing calendars set out times for fishing. For example, East Cape iwi fished for hapuka and snapper from March to May, warehou and moki in June and July, rawaru, kumu kumu (gurnard) from August to October.

Bull kelp (seaweed) was used as storage bags such as poha titi (bags to store muttonbirds in).

Fish images were used for people. For example, the people of Tauranga were Purukupenga (full net).

Nets were made from flax. There were many different nets. Examples were korohe (bag net), tarawa (conical net), purangi (bag net for lamprey), korapa (scoop or landing net for warehou), koko (scoop net for kehe), tikoko (landing net for kahawai), whakapuru (fixed-frame shrimp net), kaha (net for whitebait), toemi (hoop net for lobster).

Fish was an important way to show manaaki (hospitality) and hui and tangi (meetings and funerals).

Fish, especially kaimoana, was an important gift item. Coastal iwi exchanged fish with inland iwi for goods such as stone, berries, and birds.

Taruke koura (crayfish pots) were made from thin manuka rods. They were kept on the sea floor with a stone sinker. Divers also caught koura (crayfish, rock lobster) by hand. Koura could be preserved in fresh water for up to 7 days before it was eaten. Starfish were used as bait in pots if nothing better was around.

In rocky channels, a helper prodded a stick along to get kehe (marble fish) to swim towards a person with a net.

Evidence from middens (rubbish dumps) suggests that Maori ate stingrays.

Weirs (pa) were dams in waterways through which water could flow. They were built from stakes and lined with material such as flax. They were single fences or v-shapes. Hinaki were attached to the weirs. Eels (tuna) were also taken in nets, by spearing, by striking, and by hand.

Flounder (patiki) were speared. Lights for night fishing were made of dry leaves, bark, supplejack or kahikatea (white pine). Flounder were also caught in drag nets with sinkers to keep the nets on the bottom.

Karengo seaweed grew on rocks. It was gathered in autumn and winter. It could be eaten fresh or preserved by drying.

Shark meat could be preserved by drying. Sharks also provided oil, and teeth for tools and decoration.

Kina (spiny sea urchin) was gathered from under rocks and shelves on the shore. It could be preserved in fresh water for up to 7 days before it was eaten.

Religious ceremonies were important. Karakia (chants to bring good things and stop bad things happening) were said. The first fish caught (te ika tuatahi) was given back to the sea with a karakia.

Drying by sun preserved fish. Preserved fish was stored in pataka (storehouses on poles).

Each coastal iwi had a special seafood (kaimoana) that added to the tribe's mana. The tribe thought of their special seafood as a taonga (treasure).

Special fishing objects such as big canoes were tapu (protected, sacred).

A rahui (ban) stopped fishing in places under pressure, or fishing out of season.

Fishing was a main economic activity. Maori fishing today is still very important.

Customs (tikanga) set up fishing rules. For example body wastes were not allowed to enter the sea; baskets could never be dragged over shellfish beds.

Whitebait (inanga) were caught by weirs, hinaki, nets. They were eaten fresh or preserved by being cooked in leaf packages and then dried.

Whales stranded on the beach gave meat, oil, milk, bones, fat and teeth. Tohunga offered karakia to draw whales in to shore. Traditions told of arguments over whales between early waka groups.

Hinaki were also set in swamps.

Tangaroa was god and father of fish. Only by respecting Tangaroa and his home could people take fish.

Hooks (matau) were made from wood, bone, stone, shell.

Activities

1. A glossary is a list of special words and terms with meanings beside them. Make a Fishing Glossary. List, in alphabetical order, all the Maori terms and words to do with fishing. Put their meanings beside them.
2. The answer is flax. What are three possible questions?
3. Did early Maori use technology to help them fish? Draw up a chart like the following to show your answer.

Title:	
Evidence for:	Evidence against:
My Answer:	

4. Rule up a page into 4 sections. Choose 4 items from the text about fishing eg. pataka, shark, fish hook, light used for floundering. Put a drawing and / or information about them in your sections.
5. Research: Some fishing nets were over 1.6 km long. Find out about them.

Nuku – The Bird Hunter

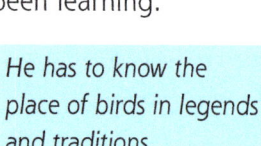

- The migration of tangata whenua is important.
- People make decisions about access to and use of resources.
- The way people manage resources has an impact on the environment.

Nuku is 14. The elders have been watching him. 'Nuku has talent,' they said. 'He has all the things that will make him a great bird hunter. He is chosen to be taught bird hunting.'

These are the things Nuku has been learning.

He has to know the place of birds in legends and traditions.	For example, who did Maui take when he went off to slay the goddess of death? He took birds, such as the fantail and whitehead.
He has to show respect to birds.	For example, he must remember that the tohunga uses birds such as the harrier (kahu) and morepork (ruru) to communicate with gods.
He has to be a conserver.	He knows that some birds have become extinct. So he must always try to keep the bird population high. He must try to draw more birds to his tribal area. This idea of making sure there will always be birds for future generations is called sustainability.
He has to be a skilful observer.	He must study the feeding habits of birds. He has to know, for example, how to set his noose snares for the tui in kowhai when the kowhai is flowering and in kahikatea when the kahikatea has berries on it. He must also watch out for signs of kiore which eat eggs and chicks.
He has to be fit.	He will set snares for pigeons at the top branches of white pine which are more than 30m above ground.
He has to be strong.	He will use spears up to 10m long to catch birds from platforms built in trees.
He has to be cunning.	He will learn to use his spear on windy or rainy days so birds can not hear him coming. He will make his snares look very old so birds will not be warned.
He has to work well with other people.	An expedition to the forest is very important. It is a lot of work involving many other people.
He has to be patient.	He has to learn to wait and do jobs such as taming birds to act as decoys. A decoy is a real or carved bird used to attract other birds so they can be trapped.
He has to follow forest rituals.	Rituals are ceremonies; they are set rules for doing jobs properly. Nuku must follow the tohunga's lead and respect that Tane is the origin of bird life. He must remember the tohunga says chants to Tane and other gods to make many birds appear. This will mean good hunting.
He has to look after hunting gear.	He must use a special whare (house) for storing and mending gear such as ladders and traps.
He has to be inventive.	Under the tohunga's supervision, he has to help invent tools and methods such as water troughs, perch snares, decoys, spears with bone points.
He has to learn how birds are preserved.	This is something else his people invented in New Zealand – how to preserve birds in fat. Birds are cooked and de-boned. A wooden trough under the cooking birds catches the fat. The birds are put into containers of kelp, gourds, totara bark. The fat is then poured over the birds.

Nuku's bird profiles

Kiwi
Likes dark parts of forest. Comes out at night. Flightless. Eats worms and grubs.

Titi
Muttonbird. Crosses oceans and makes landfall in New Zealand for breeding.

Weka
Woodhen. Thief. Flightless. Likes swamps, bush, marsh, gullies. Quick runner. Eats insects and vegetable matter. Nosey and bold.

Kakariki
Parakeet. Brightly coloured. Eats berries. Clever mimic. Fairly tame. Likes forest and bush. Active. Clambers from bough to bough, often high in treetops

Huia
Poor flight. Moves from bough to bough in trees. Likes mountain ranges and forests. Alert. Easily attracted.

Putangitangi
Duck. Likes marshes, river mouths, inland swamps, lakes. Eats fish, worms, crustacea (water creatures with shell such as crabs and water fleas.)

Pitotoi
Robin. Flits, hops, perches. Likes forest and bush. Spends a lot of time on forest floor where it gets much of its food. Tame. Easily attracted by bait on ground.

Tui
Parson bird. Eats honey, berries, insects. Roosting bird. Great mimic. Likes bush. Fast, graceful flight. Restless.

Kaka
Parrot. Noisy, active, social. Eats grubs in rotting tree trunks, among leaf mould on forest floor. Likes forest and bush. Hops on ground. Tamed kaka act as decoys.

Keruru
Pigeon. Likes bush. Loudly beating wings in flight. Colourful. Feeds almost entirely on berries, especially of miro trees. This makes them fat and thirsty.

Some of Nuku's hunting methods

A He sets snares beside water troughs high in the trees.
B He stretches nooses joined to cords across rivers and lakes.
C He sets nets near the coast on a misty night and lights fires to attract birds.
D He holds a stick out with slip noose joined to the end and slips the noose over the head.
E He sets a ground trap with bait inside.
F He builds a fern hut on the ground at the end of an 8m pole. A decoy attracts a wild bird down the pole. Nuku's hand catches it.
G He goes night hunting with dogs.
H He goes out on cold frosty nights and looks for roosting places where the bird's claws are frozen to the perch.
I He waits with a spear high in the tree tops.
J He sets a noose on the ground in a gully.

Activities

1 Make up a 10 column chart. Study Nuku's bird profiles and hunting methods. Match names of birds to methods.
2 This is a legend about how the tara kaniwha — barbed point of the spear — came about. *Maui and his bros went bird hunting with spears. Each time they speared a bird, the bird got free. Maui told his mum how hopeless the hunt had been. She told him to make a spear point with barbs. He did so. It worked.* Make a cartoon strip about this legend.
3 Discuss whether or not you have qualities that would have made you a fine bird hunter.
4 Research: Find out how early people might have hunted moa.

Working to Get Food

Focus
- The migration of tangata whenua is important.
- Producers and consumers have rights and responsibilities.
- Economic decisions have an impact on people and communities.

Different groups did different work

Group 1: Whole tribe
The tribe might work in a group under the leadership of a chief or tohunga. A tohunga was a person skilled in a particular activity. The tribe might work all together at harvesting a crop. It might cut down forest to make kumara gardens. It might build an eel weir (dam). It might steer eels along the weir to a trap. It might use a big net to catch a school of fish. If there was a big feast planned, the whole tribe helped with a hangi. They dug an oven or pit in the ground and used fire to heat stones in it. They put baskets of food on top of the stones and covered everything with earth. Food steamed for several hours.

Group 2: Males
They did work needing strength, or that was tapu. For example, they planted crops. They cut down trees. They dug up fern roots. They took canoes out to sea and fished. They harvested cabbage tree stems which women cooked to get sugar. They snared birds. Kiore were a source of protein and a special treat to give visitors. Men hunted them by putting traps along rat tracks. Traps were made of bark, flax and supplejack, and kumara was the bait. Kiore were clever at stealing food. Men built platforms or storing boxes called pataka in which to hide food for winter. The platforms and boxes sat on poles which rats could not climb.

Group 3: Females
They did less dangerous work, or less tapu work. For example, they weeded gardens. They collected items such as shellfish and berries. They cooked and preserved food.

Group 4: Slaves
They did the boring and worst jobs. For example, they carried loads. They fetched water.

Group 5: Children
They learned about kai gathering by doing jobs such as carrying. They learned rituals such as never taking cooked food into the forest. They joined in when the whole tribe was needed. A child might feed the tohunga when the tohunga was tapu and not allowed to touch food.

Group 6: Old people
They did skilled jobs that needed patience. For example, the men made tools and implements for food-gathering. Women plaited flax into round dishes called kono to hold cooked food.

Group 7: The Family
As a group, the family had the main responsibility for getting its own food. It controlled its stored food, small eel dams on small streams, small fishing canoes and some gardens, some fishing grounds and some shellfish beds. Families together making up the local community controlled big food storage pits and pataka, big eel dams on main rivers, bigger fishing canoes and fishing grounds, and the central gardens.

Group 8: Chief
He worked alongside people to set an example. He had the most responsible jobs such as dividing up food. For example, he would divide up fish so each family group got some. He got some of the first products from harvesting of crops, hunting and fishing. He had the right to stranded sea animals. He usually had more than one wife and had slaves. Therefore his household produced more food than others. He was expected to feed needy people. He provided the biggest share of hospitality given to visitors.

Group 9: Tohunga
He was a specialist but worked with the tribe when not doing specialist work. He knew that each food resource had a life force – mauri – that made it special. He might visit a tuahu – a ceremonial altar. There he would call on the gods to bless the planting of a crop and bring a good harvest. Activities such as planting kumura or hunting birds had certain rituals. Because he knew the rituals he was also regarded as a priest. He had no written instructions to refer to. Less skilled people might consult him. For example, one traditional story tells of a tohunga advising the use of cooked kumara to break a spell. Other tribes might also ask for his skills. He got gifts of food.

Group 10: Workers from another village
If there was a big job to be done, the chief might invite experts and workers from another village. The visitors were fed and given gifts to take home.

Activities

1. Make a list of food producers, and another list of food consumers. Explain your lists.
2. Explain how producers and consumers had rights (things they could expect to get) and responsibilities (things they were expected to do).
3. Work out which group of people probably did the following job. *Workers separated the inside partitions of bull kelp. They inflated the partitions to make containers (poha). Into the containers they put cooked muttonbirds. They poured in hot fat from cooking. They covered each container with totara bark. They put each poha into a kete.*
4. Make a sketch of village life to show different groups doing different activities.
5. Research: Find out what the term ohu means and how it applied to society.

Sharing Resources

Focus
- The migration of tangata whenua is important.
- People make decisions about access to and use of resources.
- Economic decisions have an impact on people and communities.
- The way people manage resources has an impact on the environment.

Maori had no money. They did not buy or sell. They did not barter or haggle. They did not even trade in the strictest sense of the word. They shared resources by exchanging gifts.

A coastal tribe might send an inland tribe a gift of dried seaweed and dried fish. It was understood but not spoken of that the inland tribe would send the coastal tribe a return gift. It might be some preserved forest birds. The inland tribe might send the gift immediately. Or it might wait weeks or months, even a year to send the gift.

The coastal tribe would never say what it wanted in return. It might drop hints. It might comment that it had heard that this was a good year for rat-trapping in the forest.

Gift exchanging was tied up with the idea of utu, or compensation. Utu is usually seen as revenge for a real or imagined crime or insult. But the idea also applied to gifts. What was needed to make the other tribe satisfied was left to the party who had received the gift.

The return gift should be at least equal in value to the original gift. Often it was larger than the original. This increased the mana of the giving tribe. Not giving a return gift would mean great loss of mana. It would also mean loss of friendship.

Gift-giving was an important part of meetings between groups. When a person died, relatives might bring important hierlooms such as a greenstone mere or a feather cloak. Sometime later, the receiver of the hierloom would return it to the giver when someone from the giver's family had died.

People also gave gifts in return for services. A chief might give a gift of food to workers or a tohunga who helped build a war canoe.

Gifts were mainly food and tools. Different environments were known for their specialities. For example, the people of Rotorua and other lakes preserved inanga (whitebait) and koura (crayfish). The people on the upper Whanganui river were famous bird hunters. They hunted by day and in the evening cooked the birds and preserved them in their own fats. The people around the Tauranga area were close to the island of Tuhua from which they got obsidian (tuhua).

Activities

1. Discuss the difference between modern trading and early Maori gift-exchanging.
2. Explain why early sites of greenstone tools and ornaments were in the South Island but greenstone tools and ornaments were also used in the North Island.
3. List things that might have been suitable for a gift-exchange. Where possible give them their Maori name.
4. Research: Find out what obsidian and greenstone look like and where they are found in New Zealand.

17 Naming the Environment

Focus
- The migration of tangata whenua is important.
- People remember and record the past in different ways.

Many of New Zealand's place-names show the earliest people's attachment to their environment.

Place names

roa = long
aka = form of whanga

koura = crayfish
kai = food

puke = hill
te = the

maru = shelter
ti = cabbage tree

tika = directly
hoki = to return

o = the place of
nehunga = burial

roto = lake
rua = two

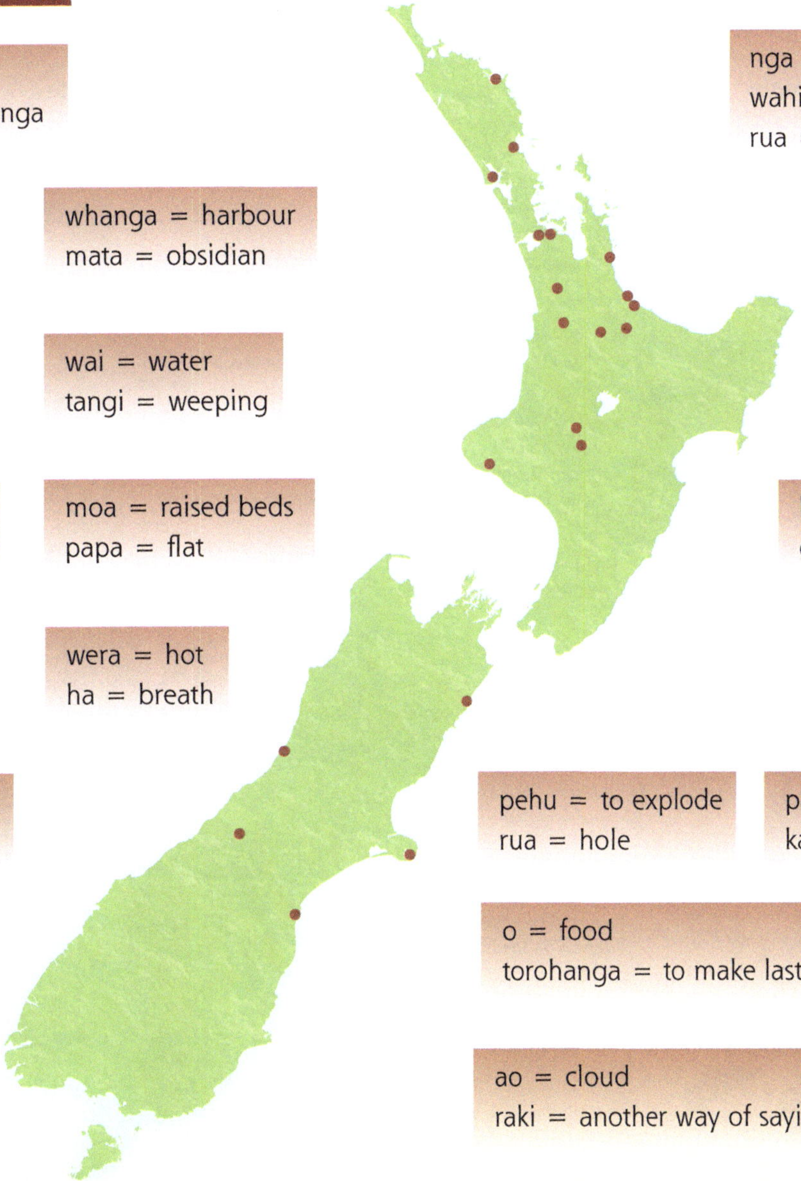

whanga = harbour
mata = obsidian

wai = water
tangi = weeping

moa = raised beds
papa = flat

wera = hot
ha = breath

nga = the
wahia = broken into
rua = holes

toko = pole
roa = long

ouru = west
wai = water

huhu = grub
ota = uncooked

one = beach
rahi = long

pehu = to explode
rua = hole

para = fern root
kai = food

o = food
torohanga = to make last for a long time

ao = cloud
raki = another way of saying rangi (=sky)

Activities

1. Make your own copy of the map. Arrange the words for each place name to get the name and then write in the name beside the place marked by a dot.
2. Discuss the link between place names, and culture and heritage.
3. Research: Hawkes Bay is believed to have one of, if not the, longest place name in the world. Find out what it is and where it got its name.

Clothes from the Land

Focus
- The migration of tangata whenua is important.
- People move between places, which has results for the people and the places.
- The way people manage resources has an impact on the environment.
- People make decisions about access to and use of resources.

Early Maori must have shivered in their new land. Their tapa cloth clothes were made from the paper mulberry plant. They were too thin. Besides, people found their paper mulberry plant did not grow well in Aotearoa. However, Aotearoa had a wonder plant of its own – flax. People learned how to use this to make warmer clothes. When a European missionary told Maori that his country of England did not grow flax, Maori could not understand how people lived without it.

Female

- Cloak pin of bone, shell or stone.
- A few have topknots like men but most wore hair short.
- Tattoo round chin and lips.
- Rarely wore combs but wore neck and ear ornaments of shell, bone or stone.
- Perfume sachet made from resin or grass.
- Flax cloak. Some capes had pompom decorations. Dyes came from bark, plants, mud. Taniko designs on the borders of flax cloaks were geometric patterns.
- Extra outer rain cloak with flax fibre as base and short strips of flax making a layer of thatch on the outside. This allowed it to shed rain.
- Basket plaited from flax or cabbage tree leaves.
- Kilt of plaited flax.
- Plaited flax sandals.

Male

- Decorative comb made from hardwood and bone with carvings and paua designs.
- Huia feather.
- Long hair done in topknot.
- Red ochre for make up.
- Neck and ear pendants.
- Tattoos.
- Cloak of flax covered with feather or strips of dogskin. There are stories of seal skin cloaks but none have been found. Some cloaks covered the whole body.
- Belt of braided grass; bunches of grass or leaves hung from belt.
- Tattoos on thighs and buttocks.
- Plaited flax sandals. Men took several pairs if they were going on a long trip.

Flax – wonder plant

Females learned how to prepare flax. They used shells to scrape away the green flesh. This left the strong fibre they called muka. They pounded muka until it was soft. They washed and sometimes dyed the muku.

Flax was like a family. The inside shoot was rito, the baby. The leaves protecting the rito were matua, the parents. The outside leaves were tupuna, the grandparents. People could cut only the tupuna. Otherwise the plant would be damaged.

The flax weaver

Know that it is an honour to be taught how to weave flax. A fine weaver brings economic gain to tribe and family. Weaving may be exchanged for food.

Cut only during the day.

Cut only the tupuna, the outer leaves.

Cut on a downward angle away from the centre of the plant so that water runs off and not into the plant.

Cut from both sides of the plant so it stays balanced.

Say a karakia (prayer) before cutting flax.

Cut only on days when there is no rain, frost or wind. Otherwise you will damage the young shoot and the leaves will be too hard to work.

Don't eat while working with flax.

Weave important clothes only during the day. If a stranger comes near, roll the flax up and cover it.

Don't cut or weave flax if you are pregnant or sick.

Don't burn flax. Make a bundle of waste material and return it to the plant to rot.

How to make a tipare headband

Preparation
Split leaves into plaiting strips by pressing the two halves of the leaf together. Slit with the thumbnail to remove the midrib and get even strips. You will need several strips of about 1.5cms in width.

Plaiting
1 Start by folding one flax strip (B1 B2) round a second flax strip (A1 A2).

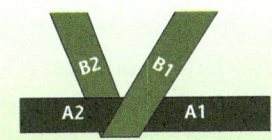

2 Fold A1 at the dots over B1. It will then look like picture 3.

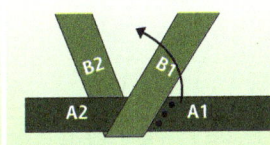

3 Fold A2 at the dots under B2 and over A1. It will then look like picture 4.

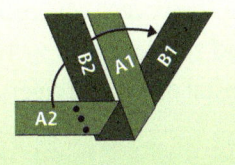

4 Fold B1 at the dots, over A2 and A1 and under B2. It will then look like picture 5.

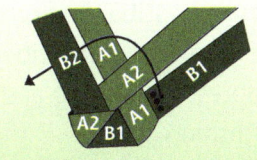

5 Fold B1 at the dots, over B2 and under A1. It will then look like picture 6.

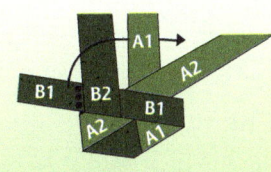

6 Fold B2 at the dots over A1 and B1 and under A2. It will then look like picture 7.

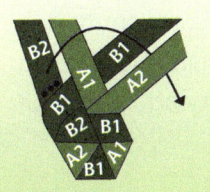

7 Fold B2 at the dots over A2 and under B1. It will then look like picture 4 again.

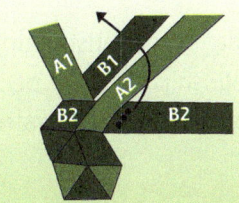

Repeat 4,5,6,7 again and again until the headband is long enough. Add new strips when they are needed by overlapping them. Tie the ends together with flax strip. Decorate with two flax pieces.

Activities

1. Discuss how traditional Maori clothes are part of New Zealand culture and heritage today.
2. Explain the link between the environment and people's management of the flax resource.
3. Describe what model you would use to show a group of Japanese tourists what clothes early Maori wore. For example, computer imaging? A clay model?
4. Explain the dress of the people here.

5. Research: Find out how to make flax sandals.

Blood and Bone Groups

Focus
- The migration of tangata whenua is important.
- Groups make decisions that impact on communities.
- People take part as individuals and as groups to respond to challenges.
- Ideas and actions of people in the past have helped shape society.

The Polynesian explorers landed at different places along the coast. Later they began to learn things like how to store food and build fortified pa. Life became more settled. The temporary camps that people set up to get food resources grew into communities and groups of people.

These were the main groups:

WHANAU	=	to give birth
HAPU	=	pregnancy
IWI	=	bone
WAKA	=	canoe

) the idea of a blood and bone tie - that they are all descended from common ancestors.

This is how the groups fitted together:

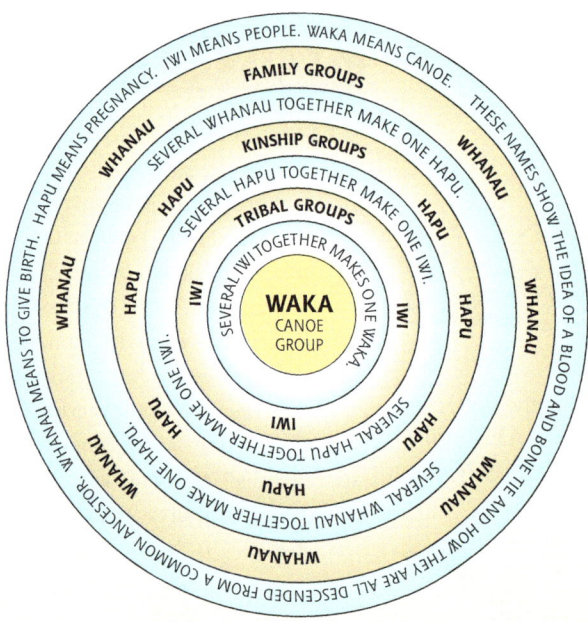

These ties were strong. The hapu might have quarrels amongst themselves; however, they would be ready to put these aside if the tribe was in danger. This way of living together as a community is called communal.

As tribes became established, so did land boundaries. Land was all-important. People said they were part of the land. It was a source of who they were. They shared it with their ancestors and with their descendants. Land boundaries identified a tribe. No individuals owned land.

The land was not densely populated. Only small parts were used for buildings and crop growing. Tribal boundaries, however, covered the whole country. Tribes had special areas such as forest for hunting and coastal areas and rivers for fishing.

As a member of a tribe, you would grow up learning about how people are organised into relationships with each other, with the land, and with the gods. You would learn how society had these groups:
- Rangatira – leaders, chiefs
- Taurekareka – slaves captured during war
- Tutua – ordinary people, biggest group
- Tohunga – specialists

Because your parents would be working hard, much of your day-to-day instruction might come from your grandparents. They would tell you practical details of the relationship between people and land. Taro needs a light soil to grow well, for example. That is why your mother and other females are carrying flax kits of sand from the beach to mix with the soil.

You might hear sayings like these which would tell you about relationships among people:
1. Marry a man with blistered hands.
2. To feed many mouths is inconvenient but at work numbers tell.
3. When in a tricky situation, stand by a chief and you won't be deserted.
4. My heroism is not individual; it is collective.
5. The priest leads and the food carriers follow.
6. When one chief dies, there's another ready to take his place.
7. To lose a child is leakage; to lose a parent is the bottom dropped out.
8. With your food basket and my food basket the people will thrive.
9. You at the handle, and I at the other handle of the basket.
10. What is the most important thing in the world? It is people!

Explanations
A The group is important.
B People are important.
C The leader is important.
D The community is important.
E Working together is important.
F The family is important.
G Hard work is important.
H Sharing is important.
I The priest is important.
J But everyone can be replaced.

You would be told about the gods and how important it was for people to keep the gods happy by offerings from the gods' special places.

Examples of gods

TANE	trees and birds	**RONGO**	peace and agriculture
TU	war	**TANGAROA**	sea and fish
TAWHIRIMATEA	winds	**HAUMIATIKETIKE**	fern root

You would learn how the tohunga, right from your birth, was a special influence on your life. At your tohi (a form of baptism) he performed a ceremony over you in flowing water. He asked Rongo or Tu to give you special physical and mental qualities. He dedicated you to the god by dunking you in water or by sprinkling you with water from a branch dipped into the water. The tohunga said karakia chants over you, like this:

Let this girl child be able to ...
- prepare food
- welcome visitors
- collect shellfish
- weave baskets
- carry firewood
- weave fine cloaks

Let this boy child be able to ....
- climb mountains
- enter forts
- stand firm in battle
- catch men
- attack sentries
- carry weapons

Activities

1. The painting of a Wanganui Pa on page 34 is said to be one of the best ever done by an early European of Maori life. Discuss what it shows of how a community works.
2. Describe the 8 groups of society and how they were linked together.
3. Check out the sayings and the explanations. Draw up a chart like this and fill it out.

Saying (number)	Explanation (letter)	Example (When is it used?)
		My cousin Mere wants to get married to lazy Toki ...

4. Name the gods to which the following refer.
   a. When bird hunters went out, the first bird taken was put aside as an offering to this god.
   b. On the battlefield, the first warrior killed was used as an offering to this god.
   c. In the cultivations, material symbols of this god were used to ensure good crops.
   d. At birth children were dedicated to this god for the arts of war.
   e. At birth children were dedicated to this god for the arts of peace.
   f. From canoes, the first fish caught was dropped into the sea as an offering to this god.
   g. While at sea, priests would call on this god to get the storm stopped.
   h. To ensure good crops, a piece of root from the bracken fern was offered to this god.
5. Your new born child is to be dedicated to a god by the priest. Make up a karakia of things you hope the priest will put in.
6. Research: Find out about the Maori creation story, starting with darkness and nothingness from which Ranginui and Papatuanuku come.

Tapu

Focus
- The migration of tangata whenua is important.
- Cultural practices.

At an early age you would be introduced to tapu. You would be warned about places, people, events, and things that are tapu. Tapu meant you should not interfere with them. For example, the maternity house in which you were born, was tapu. It had to be destroyed to stop it being dangerous to other people. The wood from it could not be used for cooking fires; it might cause terrible things, even death. The house and its contents were burned. The priest then conducted a special ceremony to take away the tapu from the site.

You would be told how the gods punished people who did not listen to the warnings. Such people had lost the protection of the gods. Disaster or death might follow. Not just to the particular person but maybe to their family, land or tribe. A tohunga was needed to lift tapu and make the place, person, event or thing noa. Noa meant it was free of tapu.

Some more examples of tapu were:
- the priest's tuahu shrine. This was outside the village in a private place.
- the chief. He was very tapu. For example, if his lips touched a drinking vessel when he drank water, the vessel must not be used by other people. A chief, or a tohunga, might be so tapu others had to feed them so food would not damage their tapu.
- the latrines (toilets) by the cliff edge.
- the burial places. These were very tapu. You would never eat food there.
- a place where a person drowned. The priest would put a rahui, a ban on fishing, there for a while.
- your kumara patch may have been made tapu and that was why you did not need a fence.
- the human head. It was the most sacred part of the body. If you scratched your head, your hand became tapu and you could not use it until it had been purified and made noa.

Activities

1. Suggest a reason for the following:
   a. A chief made his hands into a cup and water was poured in.
   b. Slaves had no tapu.
   c. Natural resources were tapu.
   d. People might blame a sickness on a breaking of tapu.
2. Explain how the ideas of tapu and noa would have helped organise society.
3. Research: Find out what wahi tapu is today and how it is important for the environment.

Taonga

Focus
- The migration of tangata whenua is important.
- People pass on and look after culture and heritage.

Although things around you are shared, there are still some special ones that members of your family have as treasure (taonga). Many of these could become part of the heritage passed down the generations.

Taonga game

- shell to scrape bark from trees to make dyes
- whizzer – wooden disc and cord spun in hands to make a noise
- patu aruhe – special fern root pounder
- toki – adze (like an axe) for working wood
- **1**
- tiki
- bone needle for sewing
- greenstone ear pendant
- nose-flute made from wood
- prized huia feathers for hair decoration
- **3**
- ko – digging tool with carved foot-rest and handle
- cloak pin made of bone
- yellow earth to burn and make red ochre war make-up
- **2**
- hanks of flax ready for weaving
- pair of carved sticks (turuturu) to hang weaving on
- two fire sticks – upper rubbing stick and lower grooved stick
- plaited belt
- piece of obsidian used for fine carving
- **4**
- cord drill (tuwiri) for drilling holes in bone and stone
- greenstone mere – most highly prized weapon
- kete – woven flax basket
- **5**
- blunt-ended long wooden spear
- decorative comb (heru)
- small flax bag to strain juice from berries
- cloak made with red feathers from kaka parrot
- mutu – bird snare and perch
- carved wooden canoe bailer (tata)
- **6**
- uhi – chisel to do tattooing
- long cord used for string games
- **7**
- tetere – flax trumpet
- calabash – gourd drinking vessel
- hoop of aka wine for rolling along ground
- **8**
- flax sleeping mat
- two-piece fishing hook made from wood and bone
- small carved box to hold feathers
- fishing net made from green flax
- **9**
- basalt chisel for carving
- **10**
- matua – collection of bone, wood, shell, stone fish hooks
- kawe – plaited back-pack
- perfume sachet filled with resin from taramea (spear) grass

RULES
1. Spin a coin on the numbered circles. The aim is to land on a circle and collect its taonga.
2. If you land across two circles, take the circle on which more than half the coin lands. If you land on a circle where the treasure has been collected, you cannot have it.
3. Play with a partner. Ten turns each. Heads spins first.

Activities
1. Play the Taonga Game. The winner is the one who collects most.
2. Discuss how the taonga you collected give clues about the type of society they came from.
3. Take part in a class competition to see who can come up with the longest list of Maori words with their meanings from all the pages up to this page.
4. Research: Find out about mokomokai – preserved heads.

Problem Solving 1

Focus
- The migration of tangata whenua is important.
- Exploration creates chances and challenges for people, places, and environments.
- Events have causes and effects.
- People move between places, which has results for the people and the places.

> Problem = How to make tough, long-lasting tools.
> Solution = Use materials at hand such as wood, bone and stone.

The tribes had no knowledge of metal. They experimented with new stones they found. They set up quarries and tool-making places. They used stones such as argyllite, andesite, greywacke, and basalt to make knives, chisels, axes and hammers. On the west coast of the South Island, they found a special stone. This was pounamu (greenstone). It was tough and strong. Yet other stones such as sandstone and greywacke could shape it.

Methods of tool making

1 Flaking or chipping. The sharp edge flake might be the tool needed. Or the core itself might be chipped into an adze.

2 Battering or picking. This is breaking down the stone by hitting it lightly and constantly with a hammer.

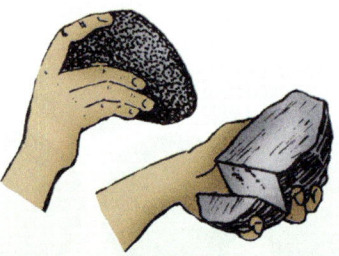

3 Grinding. This is grinding the stone smooth on a piece of sandstone.

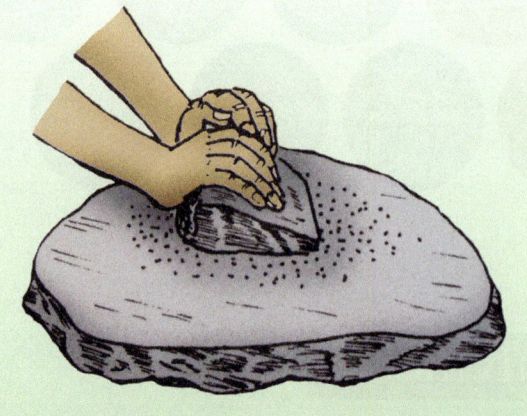

4 Cutting or sawing. This is done by a mania which is a blunt stone tied onto a stick or held in the hand. It is often used with wet, fine sand. The stone to be cut is ground down. A deep cut is made on each side. Then the break is made.

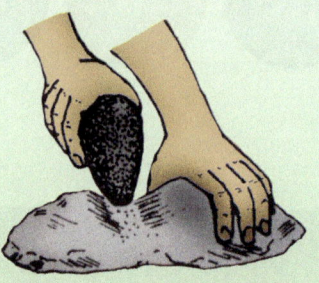

Using a stone age technology, people made every kind of tool, weapon and implement they needed for survival.

The ko was the most important gardening tool. It was a digging stick used to break up ground. It was given a foot-rest. This was an improvement on the design brought from Hawaiki. Some ko were highly carved. There were many types of spades (kaheru), and tools for special jobs such as hoeing, breaking up clods, raking. The timo, for example, was a wooden grubber for loosening soil. It was shaped like a boomerang.

Obsidian (volcanic glass known as mata) or a mussel shell (kuku) made sharp cuts used for trimming hair or making fine carving.

Whao were straight-edged chisels and round-edged gouges. A nephrite chisel might have a hole at the end so the user could wear it as an ear ornament. This would keep it safe.

The drill was made of a wooden shaft, stone point, pulling cords and balance weight. It could put a hole in a big stone to make a canoe anchor (punga) or a small stone to make a whistle (nguru).

The toki (stone adze) was king of the tools. The axe-head was lashed to the handle. Toki ranged in size from the big toki which cut down trees to the tiny ones which did delicate carving.

Activities

1. Match the picture, name and description of the tools and things the tools helped to make. (Refer to page 37 also.)

Sketch Number	Name	Description Letter

Names

mata	tata	tuwiri	timo
kuku	uhi	whao	ko
toki	patu 1	punga	heru
matua	patu 2	nguru	turuturu

Descriptions

A tattooing comb made like a tiny adze with a bone blade tied to it
B wooden pounder for pounding fern root on a stone
C fish hooks made from bone, wood, shell and stone; they often are two pieces joined together
D axe made from stone blade tied to wood handle
E digging tool used in kumara gardens
F weaving sticks about 44-56cms long; sometimes carved, have knob at one end and sharp point for putting into ground, at other end
G chisels and gouges are 2-20cms long
H anchor made of large stone with hole drilled through it for rope
I cord drill for drilling holes in stone, bone and shell; shaft is 30-60cms long and is balanced with stones tied to it; stone flake is tied to drill for point
J whistle made from wood with inside bored by drill and several holes drilled from outside, shaped so there are fat and slim ends
K comb to dress hair and be decorative; most valuable sort made from whalebone in one piece with small human head carved on side
L bailer has wide carved rim and handle jutting off it; if it belongs to an important canoe it is given a personal name
M stone pounder for pounding flax fibre
N grubber made of wood and used to loosen soil
O obsidian used for cutting, scraping and fine carving
P mussel shell used for cutting

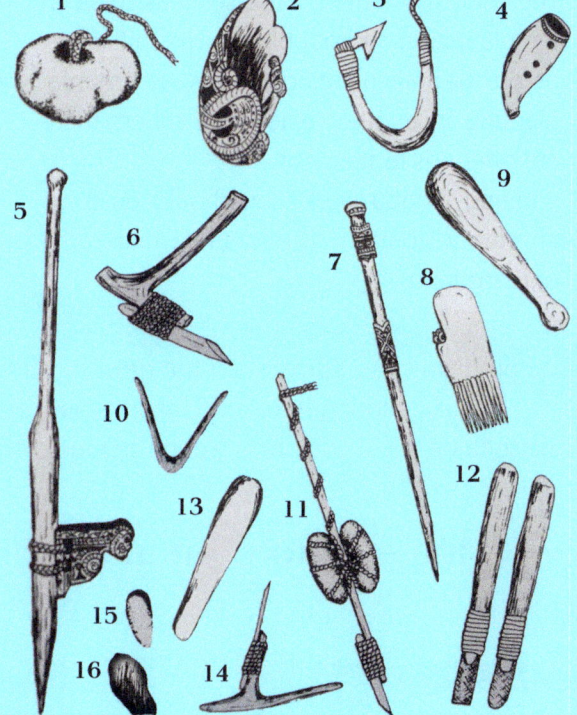

2. You live in 18th century Aotearoa. You are to pack this kete with tools as a time capsule and leave it under a heap of stones in a cave. Name the ten objects you will put in it.

3. Research: The Maori name for the South Island is Te Wai Pounamu. Find out more about greenstone.

Problem Solving 2

Focus
- The migration of tangata whenua is important.
- Exploration creates chances and challenges for people, places, and environments.
- Events have causes and effects.
- People make decisions about access to and use of resources.

Long before you were old enough to work in the cultivations, you would have started to learn things about the kumara, such as:

- it is the most important cultivated food brought from Hawaiki.
- it is called 'Treasure from Hawaiki'.
- it is an excellent food.
- it is grown from tubers saved from the last crop.
- there is more population growth in places the kumara does well.
- planting season is September/October.
- Mahura (Spring) will send the cuckoo from Hawaiki when it is time to plant.

Later on, you will learn more details, such as:

- the kumara caterpillar eats kumara leaves. The tribe has tamed some seagulls to sit in the plantation and gobble the caterpillars.
- before the main planting, there is a ceremonial planting in another place. The tubers there are offerings to the gods.
- planting is tapu work. You should do it on an empty stomach. The tohunga makes the gardens tapu.
- kumara has a mauri (life force). To look after the mauri, people put some stone images of gods in the gardens.
- the tohunga lifts the tapu at harvest time in March. The first kumara are set aside for the gods. A hakari (feast) is held.

The problem = Kumara did not grow in winter in New Zealand. People had to find a way of storing it for food, and keeping seed tubers to plant out next year.

The solution = use underground storage by digging a rua – a pit or hole.

Rua – a store pit in the ground

- Ground level
- Wooden door that seals rua, keeps kumara in dark, keeps out rats and rain.
- Kumara is kept at regular temperatures and high level of humidity.
- Lined with ferns to keep kumara dark, dry, and warm.

Activities

1. The event is the building of a rua. Describe the causes and the effects.
2. Explain why your tribe has put some wooden pegs with carved heads, and a preserved head on a post, in the ground of the kumara gardens.
3. Discuss what this proverb might mean: E kore te kumara e korero mo tona ake reka. (The kumara does not say how sweet it is.)
4. Research: Find out how early Maori prepared kumara for eating.

Health

Focus
- The migration of tangata whenua is important.
- Cultural practices.

In many ways the lifestyle was healthy. Water was the main drink. Getting enough food to eat kept people active. There were no great epidemics.

However, some features of the lifestyle were not so healthy. Examples were wars, the amount of time spent in cold water, the damage to teeth through the chewing of fernroot.

Warning: Do not attempt any of them without medical advice.

Some health remedies

Sore/weak eyes: Use drops of rata sap in them.

Toothache: Chew leaves, root of kawakawa.

Ulcers: Apply poultice of leaves and shoots of koromiko.

Warts: Cut them down.

Boils: Cut and squeeze.

Stomach upsets: Chew young leaf ends of koromiko.

Bowel upsets: Boil manuka bark and drink liquid.

Burns and scalds: Apply toetoe plumes or ashes of burned tussock grass or inner bark of rimu.

Bad battle wounds: Apply plaster of mud or dressing of plumes of toetoe or flax gum or titoki oil.

Very bad battle wounds: Apply burning firestick of karaeo (supplejack).

Sore, scratched feet: Heat leaves of paewhenua and apply to feet.

Headache: Apply inner bark of pohutukawa

Sore throat: Take nectar from rata flowers.

Choking: Recite a chant and smack patient on back.

Near drowning: Hold body up by heels over smoky fire. Cause water to run out and patient to sneeze.

Ringworm (tinea): Make cuts on flesh. Rub into cuts liquid made by boiling manuka bark and pouring it over wood ashes.

Fractures: Make splints of thick flax leaves or rata bark.

Constipation: Have infusion of manuka bark. Infusion = water in which something has been soaked.

Diarrhoea: Have infusion of manuka seed capsules.

Bleeding: Apply inner bark of pohutukawa.

Postnatal pains: Sit in oven of hot stones covered with leaves and mats.

Flesh wounds: Apply sap of rata.

Joint diseases: Squeeze and apply juice of waoriki.

A person might fall sick after he or she had broken a tapu. The tohunga did an exorcism (got rid of) of the spirit that had possessed the person. He would dip the person in a stream and say a karakia. Or he might touch the person with a karamu leaf and then let the leaf float downstream. The spirit would thus be carried off to sea and eventually to the underworld.

Activities

1. Discuss whether obesity was likely to have been a problem in early Maori society.
2. Describe how your job as tohunga is a mix of spiritual and physical healing.
3. Explain how the generally healthy lifestyle had risks.
4. Research: Find out the place of Maori herbal healing in society today.

Pa, War, Weapons

Focus
- The migration of tangata whenua is important.
- Exploration creates chances and challenges for people, places, and environments.
- Events have causes and effects.
- People move between places, which has results for the people and the places.

The first people were possibly peace-loving. If they did argue, they would have been able to pack up camp and go somewhere else.

The first villages to grow out of camps were kainga. These were open and unfortified.

As tribes became settled and attached to their land, the desire and need to defend it led to the fortified pa. They might be just big enough for a whanau, or be big enough for a whole tribe of several hundred people.

People might not live in the pa all the time. They might go away fishing or hunting for rats. The pa was there for them to shelter in during an attack. It was also a safe place to store food. It could be a centre for learning.

The pa was a mixture of the natural features of the environment and constructed defences. It was designed to slow attackers down and allow defenders to see attackers.

Natural features
- hills and scarps (steep slopes)
- cliffs
- islands
- coastal headlands
- volcanic cones

Inside the pa
- marae
- whare (houses)
- chief's whare
- rua, pataka

Constructed defences
- pallisade (high wooden fence)
- fosse (ditch)
- rampart (raised terrace)
- throwing stage
- lookout tower for sentries to recite alarms through the night to warn off raiders.

Some rituals before war party left on a raid
- war dance (haka)
- warriors bit cross-bar of latrine while tohunga recited karakia
- warriors entered stream where tohunga sprinkled them with water from branch.

How to make a greenstone mere weapon
Grind greenstone into shape out of a rough slab by rubbing it on a block of sandstone with water. Make a hole in the handle with a wooden drill and fine sand.
NOTE: The mere may not be finished in one generation's lifetime. It may have to be passed on unfinished to the next generation.

Activities

1. Sketch a pa and label its features.
2. Discuss what the picture on this page is about.
3. Describe possible reasons for the following:
   a. The bow and arrow was not used for fighting in New Zealand but was in other Polynesian cultures.
   b. The elaborately fortified pa was not known in Polynesia but became very important in New Zealand.
   c. The most elaborate pa were built on hills with fertile valleys.
   d. Captives from other tribes were killed and eaten, or turned into slaves.
4. Research: Payment (utu) for an insult was a common cause of a war party setting out on a raid. Find out about this and also the usual number of warriors in a war party.

Mana of warriors
- Warrior who killed first in battle and was able to shout 'I have the first fish' got much mana.
- The eating of dead enemy chiefs lessened their mana. The feud (quarrel) that this action started could be passed down the generations.

Some fighting methods
- hand-to-hand fighting
- formations eg. wedge formation where the best warrior was the point
- tricks eg. draw defenders out by pretend attack and lead them into planned ambush.

Some weapons
- taiaha: wooden striking, thrusting weapon, 1.5-2.5m long, carved end
- tewhatewha: wooden striking weapon, 1.5-2m long, flat axe-like end, bunch of feathers on lower part of blade to trick enemy
- greenstone mere: striking weapon, about 40cm long, flat thin-edged blade
- patu onewa: striking weapon, stone club, thick and heavy
- flesh ripper: ripping weapon, wooden, carved, shaped with row of shark teeth along edge to make blade, coloured with red ochre, paua shell for decoration
- hoeroa: throwing weapon, club, made from jaw of whale, 1.5-2m long, long cord on end to get it back after throwing.

Games and Sports

Focus
- The migration of tangata whenua is important.
- Cultural practices.

People had to work hard to survive. However, there was time for games and sport. Many of these were learning activities. They gave training in physical and mental skills.

The environment provided the playing areas and materials.

Whai (string figures)
The player stretched between the hands a 2m cord with ends spliced together. Fingers worked the cord to make figures and patterns. Some were complicated. They needed help from someone else. The player could use toes or teeth. In a competition, two players sat back to back. They started to make a design at the same time. The winner was the first finished.

Koruru (knucklebones)
Players used five pebbles in set moves for picking them up. In a competition the winner was the one who went furthest in the set moves.

Karetao (puppet)
This was a human figure carved from wood. It was about 35cm long. It stood on a round base. Arms were joined to the body with a knotted cord. The player pulled the cord to make the arms move. By shaking the karetao at the base, the player got it doing a haka. Special songs could be made up to go with the haka.

Potaka (tops)
Whip tops were made of wood, stone or pumice. Humming tops were made of gourds. Players used flax whips. Whip tops had small shells set in them to cut other tops to pieces. Players put tops inside a circle and whipped them with flax whips to get tops to fight; the aim was to push the other top out of the circle.

Teka (dart throwing)
The dart was a dry fern stalk. It had a piece of green flax tied at the thick end to make a knob. In a competition, the winner was the first to score ten longest throws.

Ti rakau (stick game)
Sticks were 1m long. Players, numbering 2 to 40, knelt in a circle. Each had two sticks. They beat the sticks together, threw one, then the other, to the person on the right who had to catch them. In a competition the player who dropped a stick fell out. The winner was the last one left in the circle.

Moari
A tall pole was put up near a river or lake. Flax ropes were attached to the top. Players swung out on a rope and dropped off into the water. A moari could be set up where there was no water. It could also be a tree.

Ti ringa (hand game)
Two players faced each other. Both beat on their thighs until the starter made a quick movement such as jerking both hands towards the right or left. The other player had to make a move at the same time. If player 2 made the same move as player 1, player 2 scored two points. If player 2 did not make the same move, player 1 scored two points. The first to ten won.

Pou toti (stilts)
Stilts for younger children were made from a straight branch with a side branch cut off to make a foot rest. Older children and adults had poles with footrests lashed on. Players used them for crossing streams, wrestling, or running races.

Pirori (hoop)
It was made with aka vine. Two players rolled it back and forward between them.

Retireti (tobogganing)
The player used a cabbage tree leaf head to slide down a hill.

Piu (skipping)
Two players held a flax rope between them for one or more players to skip it.

Poi (dancing)
The poi was made from raupo down and covered with flax or raupo leaves. It was tied into a ball with a cord. Tufts of dog hair decorated it. The player held the cord in the right hand and the left hand twirled and hit it.

Spear throwing
Spears were made of bracken fern with flax-bound ends, or from wood with blunt ends. They were about 2m long. One player threw, the other avoided it by dodging, turning it aside or catching it.

Other activities include haka, diving (always feet first), swimming, canoe racing, running, jumping, boxing, wrestling, acrobatics (standing on head, somersaulting).

Manu aute (kite flying)
Kites had no tails. Common materials used were raupo or toetoe stalks tied with strips of flax. Some had decorations of feathers. The usual shapes were crosses, human faces and birds. Some of the larger kites for adults had wingspans of up to four metres. It was said such kites could lift men into the air.

Activities

1. Make your own copy of this environment. Decide good sites for each activity mentioned. Give each activity a grading:
   * very simple
   ** needs some skill
   *** needs a range of skills
   **** needs considerable skills

2. These are some members of Nuku's extended family. They all have favourite games or sports. Make up a chart like this to show the activity/activities each member would probably prefer. The third column is for a brief reason.

Name	Activity	Reason
Cousin Mara	Ti rakau	She likes being able to sit...

Grandfather Waka Still fit, determined none of his grandsons will shame him on the battlefield.	**Granny Hinga** Mentally alert, but suffers from painful joints.	**Cousin Rangi** Eight-years-old, is fascinated by changing shapes and patterns.	**Aunty Ra** Not strong, but graceful.	**Brother Kere** Nine-years-old, thinks of nothing but becoming a famous warrior.
Cousin Mara A young adult, but a swimming accident two years ago left her physically disabled.	**Brother Ari** A young adult who has always been a speedster.	**Sister Pae** Five-years-old, always on the go, has a limited concentration span.	**Brother Pike** Only six but already competitive.	**Cousin Toka** He is an expert bird hunter who has spent years studying the flight patterns of birds.

3. Research: Find a story involving a game or sport. For example, how did Nukupewapewa, a Ngati Kahungunu chief, use a giant raupo kite to help him capture Maungarake pa?

Art

Focus
- The migration of tangata whenua is important.
- Cultural practices.

The basic art techniques and designs brought from Polynesia and then changed in New Zealand were:
- carving on wood, bone, stone
- tattooing on people
- plaiting and weaving geometric designs like the taniko borders on flax cloaks
- kowhaiwhai paintings on wood
- paintings on rocks
- tukutuku stitched panels between carvings in a meeting house.

Skill at carving came with the early Polynesians but developed in a big way in the new homeland. New Zealand had totara wood which was straight-grained and easy to carve. It also had greenstone.

People had much respect for a tohunga whakairo (carver). Far-off tribes might ask for his services. Carving was a tapu job. Females could not be near when the carver worked. The chips left over from carving were burned in a special fire.

The main design was the human figure. Some had distorted heads. The body was usually shortened. It may be that the natural human shape did not fit the size of timber used, for example, in building. Sometimes other shapes were carved such as spirals, sea monsters, birds, fish, lizards.

Traditional Patterns

Pitau (Scroll)

Koru

Ngutu kaka (crescent)

Manawa (heart)

Maori tattoo was called moko. Instead of the usual Polynesian tattoo where the pattern was pricked in, Maori cut the pattern into the flesh. Men might have a fully tattooed face and tattoos on the buttocks and thighs, and occasionally on other parts of the body such as the chest. Women were usually tattooed only on the lips and the chin. The tattooing chisel was usually from a bone of the albatross or human. The tattooist struck it with a light hammer. The pigment was usually soot got from burning kahikatea (white pine).

Tukutuku were the stitched panels between the carvings in a meeting house. Men made the panels from toetoe and fern stalks. They tied these together into small squares. Females prepared pingao (sea grass) and kiekie for stitching. They stitched the pattern through the panels. One female sat in front of the panel and another sat behind the panel.

Some traditional patterns are:

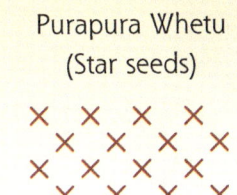
Purapura Whetu
(Star seeds)

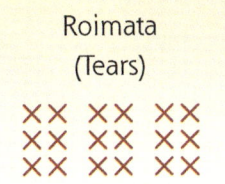
Roimata
(Tears)

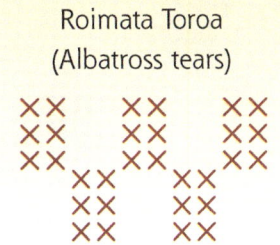
Roimata Toroa
(Albatross tears)

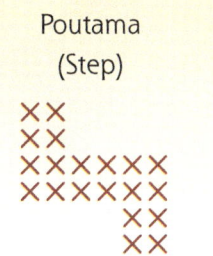
Poutama
(Step)

Taniko was the ornamental border of a woven cloak or mat.

Activities

1. Discuss how important art is to culture and heritage.
2. Decide which of the art forms you would have been good at. Be ready to say why.
3. Go back to the list of Maori words and their meanings you made in 21 Taonga. Take part in another class competition for the most words from the Taonga unit to the Art unit.
4. Research: Find two illustrations for each of the art forms mentioned.

Your Own Enquiry

Focus
- The migration of tangata whenua is important.
- Exploration creates chances and challenges for people, places, and environments.
- Events have causes and effects.
- People move between places, which has results for the people and the places.
- Ideas and actions of people in the past have helped shape people's lives.

Enquiry = finding out about a specific topic and presenting the results of your enquiry for marking.

Tangata Whenua pieces

SWINGS · KORERO (SPEECHES) · EDUCATION · MUSICAL INSTRUMENTS · TRAVEL · LOCAL MAORI SETTLEMENT · TREES · DEATH AND BURIAL · PURAKAU (STORIES) · WAIATA (SONGS)

Activities

1. Make your own copy of the Tangata Whenua pieces and put them together to make one of the earliest inhabitants.
2. Choose the title of one of the pieces to make an enquiry about. It should be on life before the arrival of Europeans.
3. Make up several questions to help you collect information. For example, if your enquiry was about travel: What sort of canoes did Maori build? How big were they? What were the sails made of? What were the war canoes like? How did they get up and down steep cliffs?
4. Make a plan for how you will get information. For example: I will use the net. I will talk to local kaumatua.
5. Keep all your information together. Write information in your own words. Decide which information you will use. For example: I will use two of the five illustrations I have found because they show pre-European canoes.
6. Prepare your enquiry for marking. Include a comment about how well it went. Hand in your enquiry.